Buffy
THE
HIGH SCHOOL
YEARS

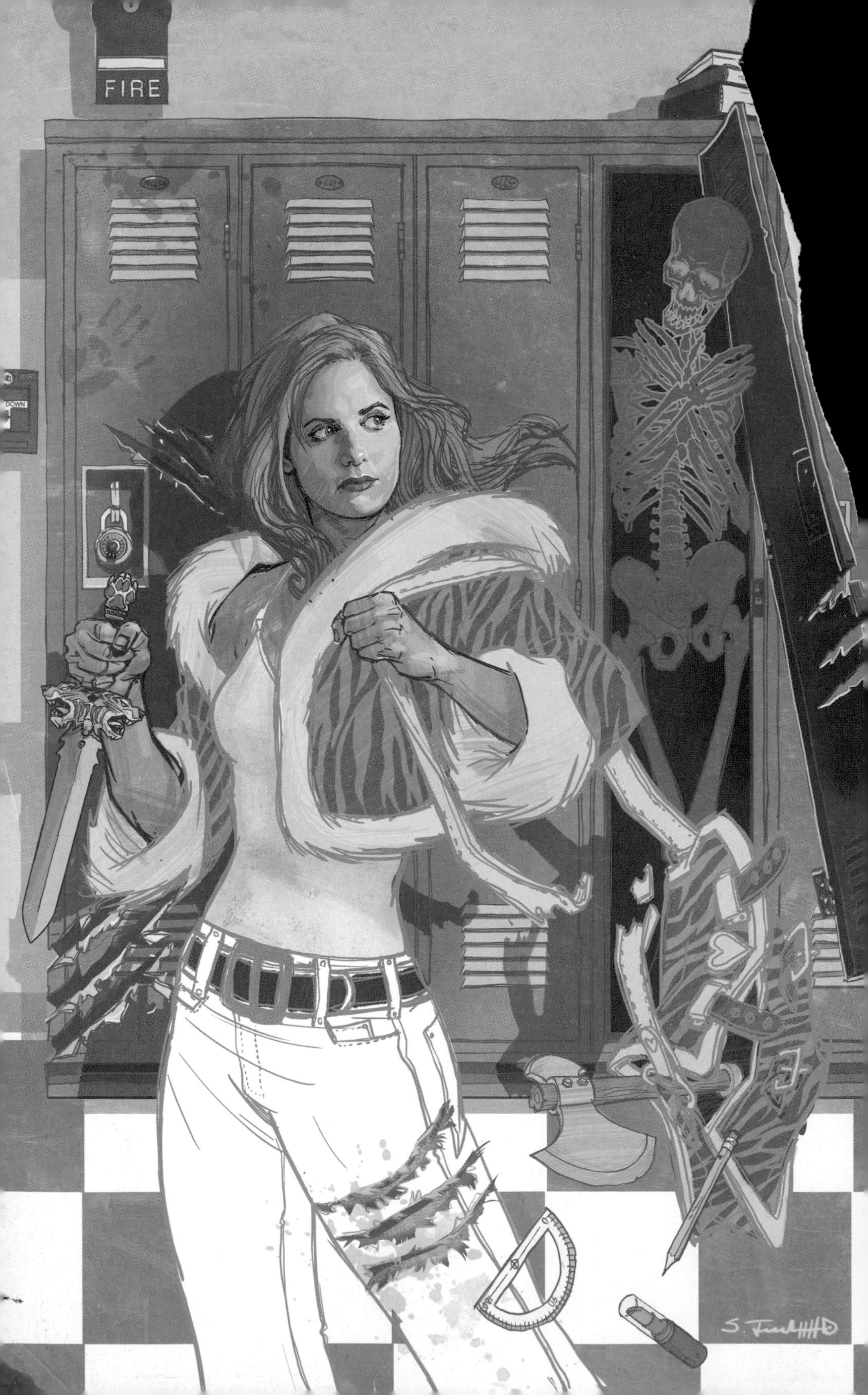
FIRE
DOWN

Buffy

THE HIGH SCHOOL YEARS

GLUTTON FOR PUNISHMENT

SCRIPT
KEL McDONALD

ART
YISHAN LI

COLORS **ROD ESPINOSA**
& TONY GALVAN

LETTERING
RICHARD STARKINGS & COMICRAFT'S
JIMMY BETANCOURT

COVER ART **SCOTT FISCHER**

EXECUTIVE PRODUCER **JOSS WHEDON**

DARK HORSE BOOKS

President & Publisher
MIKE RICHARDSON

Editor
FREDDYE MILLER

Designer
JUSTIN COUCH

Digital Art Technician
CHRISTIANNE GOUDREAU

Special thanks to Nicole Spiegel and Josh Izzo at Twentieth Century Fox,
Daniel Kaminsky, Becca J. Sadowsky, and Kevin Burkhalter.

This story takes place during *Buffy the Vampire Slayer* Season 1, created by Joss Whedon.

First edition: October 2016 | ISBN 978-1-50670-115-8 | 10 9 8 7 6 5 4 3 2 1

Published by Dark Horse Books, a division of Dark Horse Comics, Inc.
10956 SE Main Street, Milwaukie, OR 97222 | DarkHorse.com

Neil Hankerson Executive Vice President · Tom Weddle Chief Financial Officer · Randy Stradley Vice
President of Publishing · Michael Martens Vice President of Book Trade Sales · Matt Parkinson Vice
President of Marketing · David Scroggy Vice President of Product Development · Dale LaFountain
Vice President of Information Technology · Cara Niece Vice President of Production and Scheduling
· Nick McWhorter Vice President of Media Licensing · Ken Lizzi General Counsel · Dave Marshall
Editor in Chief · Davey Estrada Editorial Director · Scott Allie Executive Senior Editor · Chris Warner
Senior Books Editor · Cary Grazzini Director of Specialty Projects · Lia Ribacchi Art Director · Vanessa
Todd Director of Print Purchasing · Matt Dryer Director of Digital Art and Prepress · Mark Bernardi
Director of Digital Publishing · Sarah Robertson Director of Product Sales · Michael Gombos Director
of International Publishing and Licensing

To find a comics shop in your area, call the Comic Shop Locator Service toll-free at (888) 266-4226.
International Licensing: 503-905-2377

Library of Congress Cataloging-in-Publication Data

Names: McDonald, Kel, author. | Li, Yishan, illustrator. | Espinosa, Rod,
   illustrator. | Galvan, Tony, illustrator. | Starkings, Richard,
   illustrator. | Betancourt, Jimmy, illustrator. | Fischer, Scott M.,
   illustrator. | Whedon, Joss, 1964- producer.
Title: Buffy, the high school years : glutton for punishment / script, Kel
   McDonald ; art, Yishan Li ; colors, Rod Espinosa and Tony Galvan ;
   lettering, Richard Starkings & Comicraft's Jimmy Betancourt ; cover art,
   Scott Fischer ; executive producer, Joss Whedon.
Other titles: Glutton for punishment
Description: First edition. | Milwaukie, OR : Dark Horse Books, 2016.
Identifiers: LCCN 2016021859 | ISBN 9781506701158 (paperback)
Subjects: LCSH: Vampires--Comic books, strips, etc. | BISAC: COMICS & GRAPHIC
   NOVELS / Horror.
Classification: LCC PN6728.B84 B7 2016 | DDC 741.5/973--dc23
LC record available at https://lccn.loc.gov/2016021859

Buffy THE HIGH SCHOOL YEARS

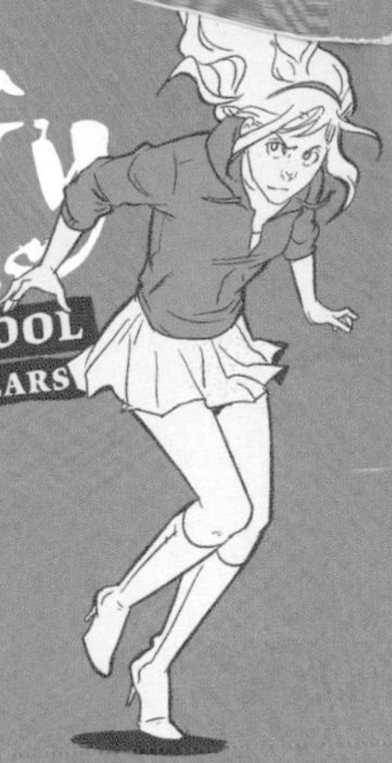

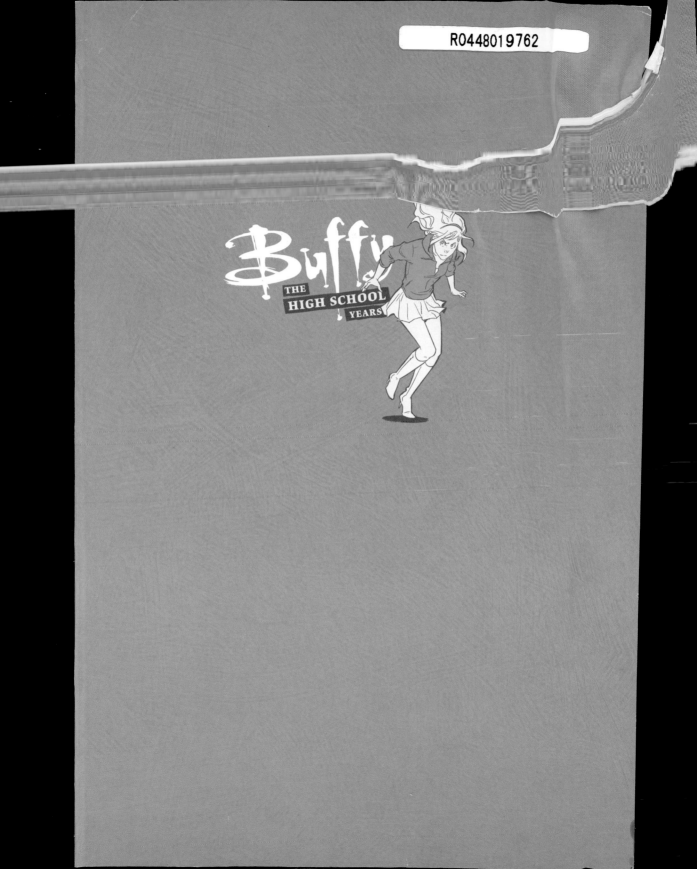

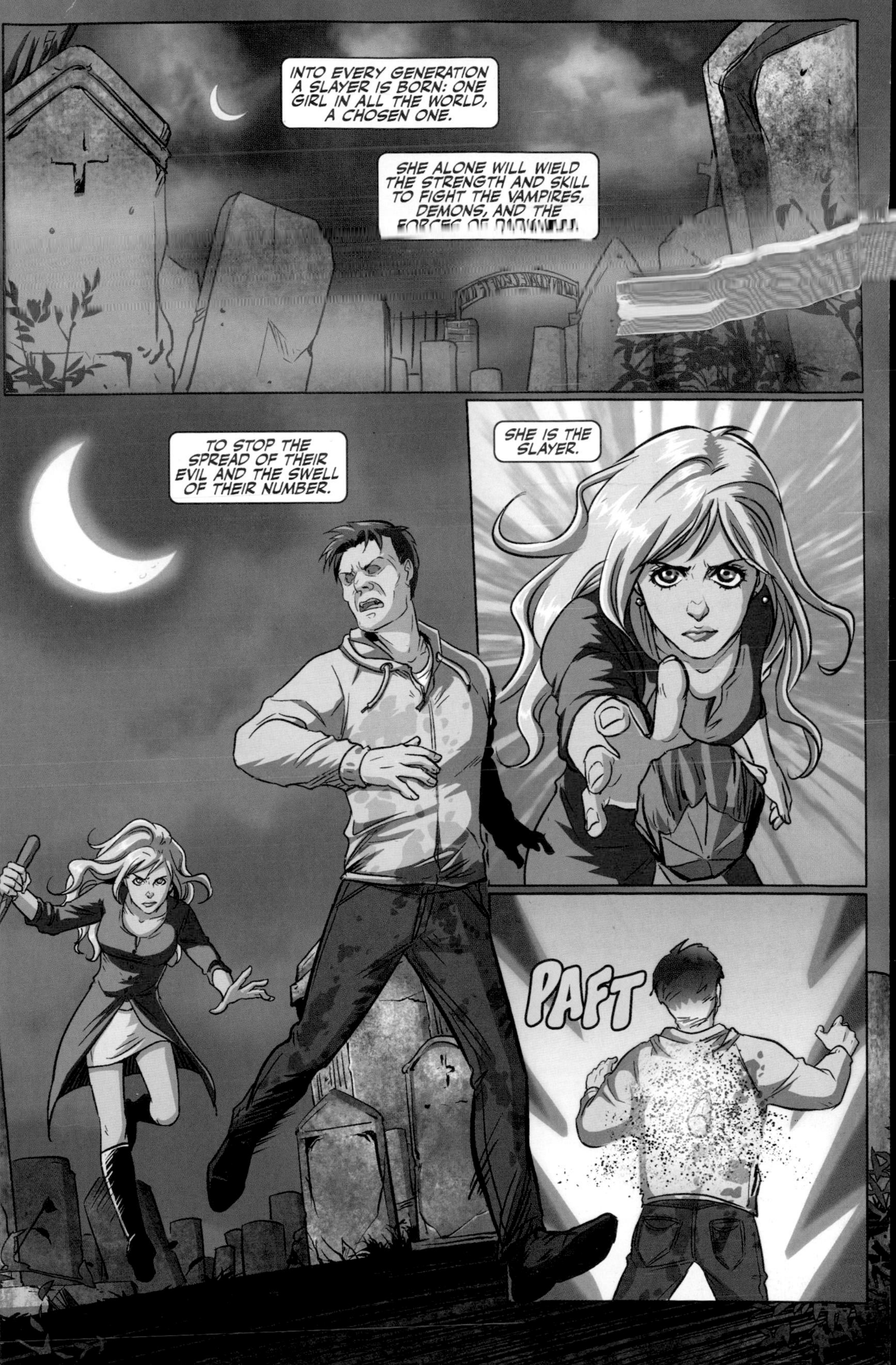
INTO EVERY GENERATION A SLAYER IS BORN: ONE GIRL IN ALL THE WORLD, A CHOSEN ONE.
SHE ALONE WILL WIELD THE STRENGTH AND SKILL TO FIGHT THE VAMPIRES, DEMONS, AND THE FORCES OF
TO STOP THE SPREAD OF THEIR EVIL AND THE SWELL OF THEIR NUMBER.
SHE IS THE SLAYER.
PAFT

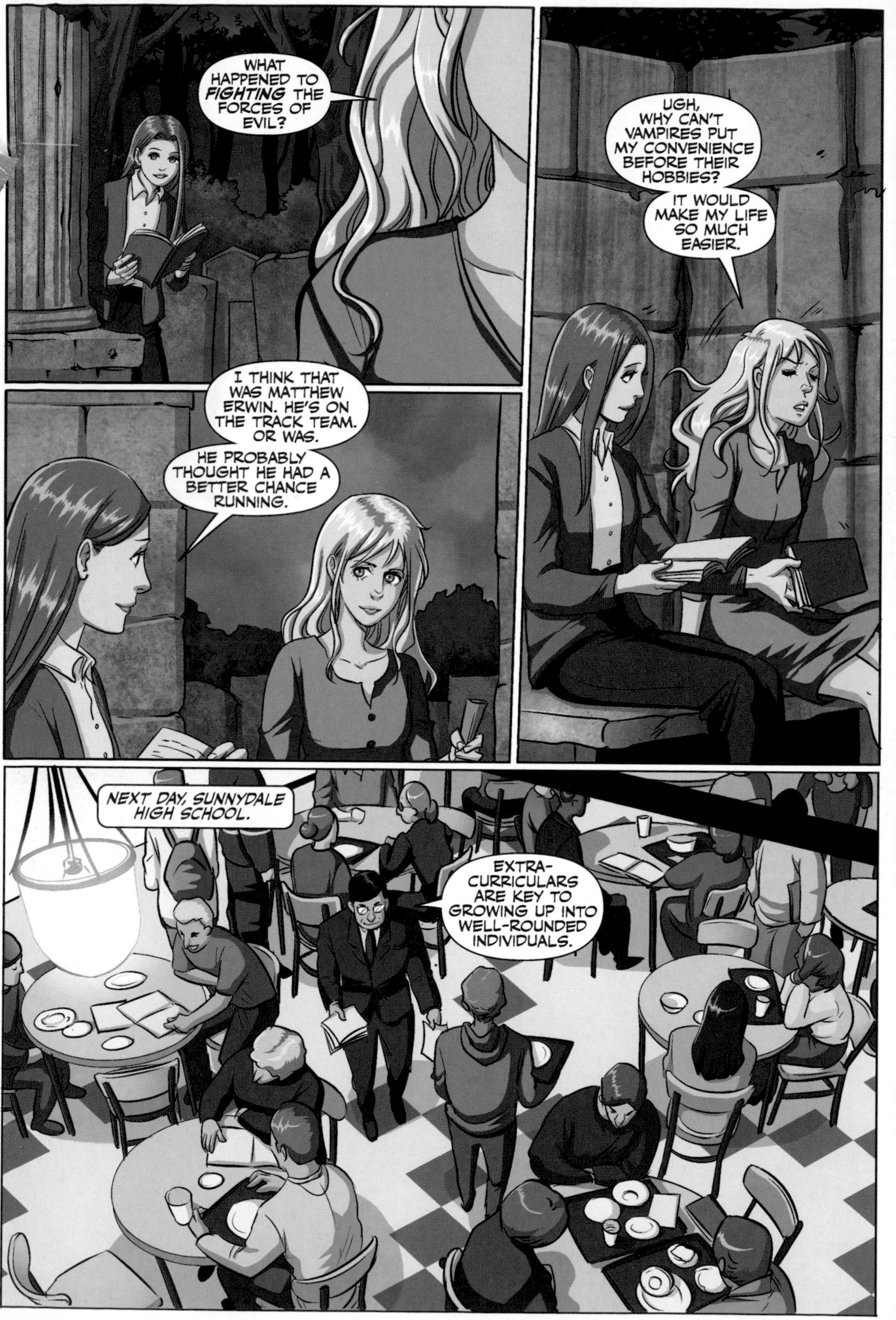
WHAT HAPPENED TO *FIGHTING* THE FORCES OF EVIL?
UGH, WHY CAN'T VAMPIRES PUT MY CONVENIENCE BEFORE THEIR HOBBIES?
IT WOULD MAKE MY LIFE SO MUCH EASIER.
I THINK THAT WAS MATTHEW ERWIN. HE'S ON THE TRACK TEAM. OR WAS.
HE PROBABLY THOUGHT HE HAD A BETTER CHANCE RUNNING.
NEXT DAY, SUNNYDALE HIGH SCHOOL.
EXTRA-CURRICULARS ARE KEY TO GROWING UP INTO WELL-ROUNDED INDIVIDUALS.

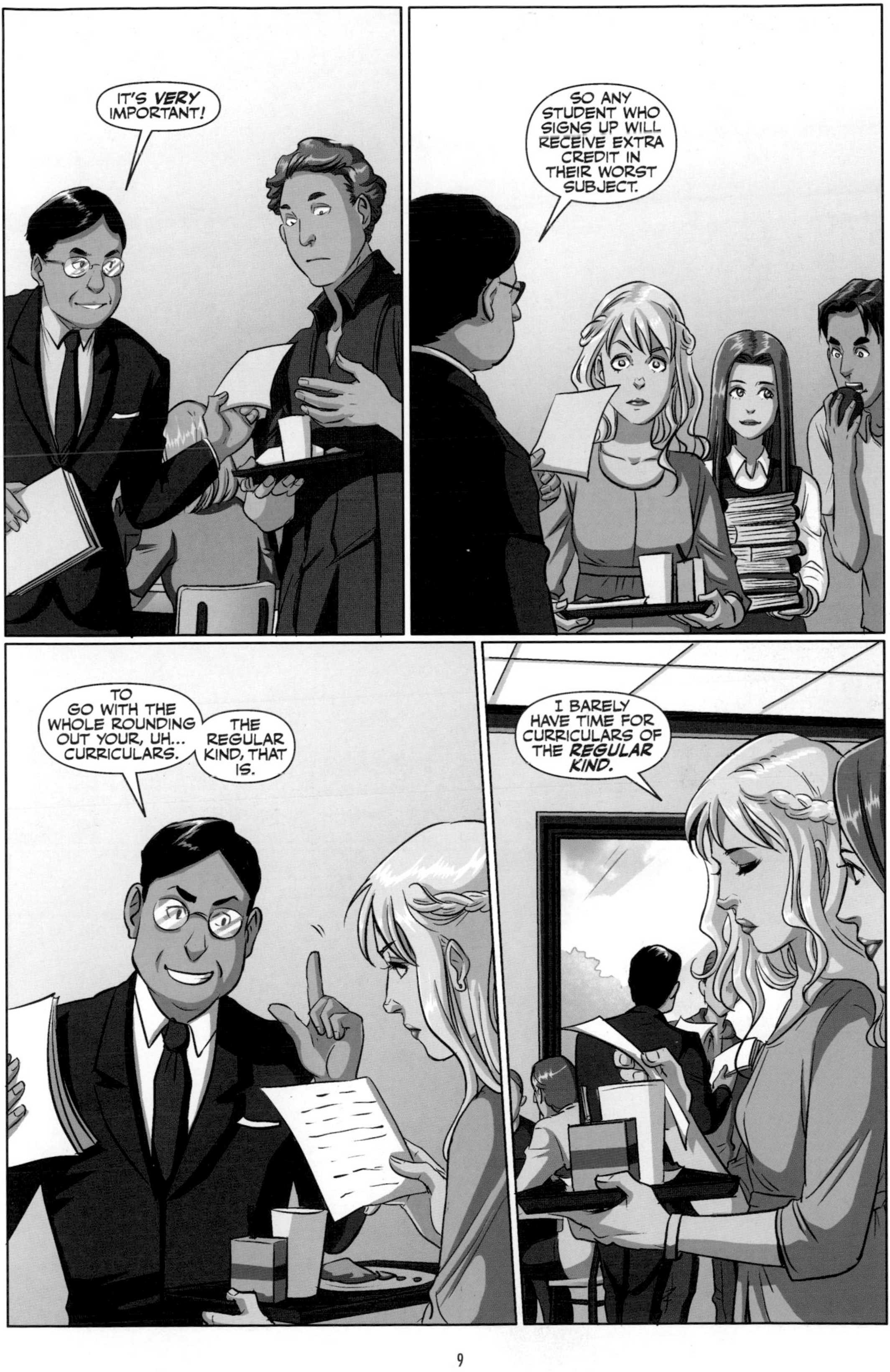
IT'S VERY IMPORTANT!
SO ANY STUDENT WHO SIGNS UP WILL RECEIVE EXTRA CREDIT IN THEIR WORST SUBJECT.
TO GO WITH THE WHOLE ROUNDING OUT YOUR, UH... CURRICULARS.
THE REGULAR KIND, THAT IS.
I BARELY HAVE TIME FOR CURRICULARS OF THE REGULAR KIND.

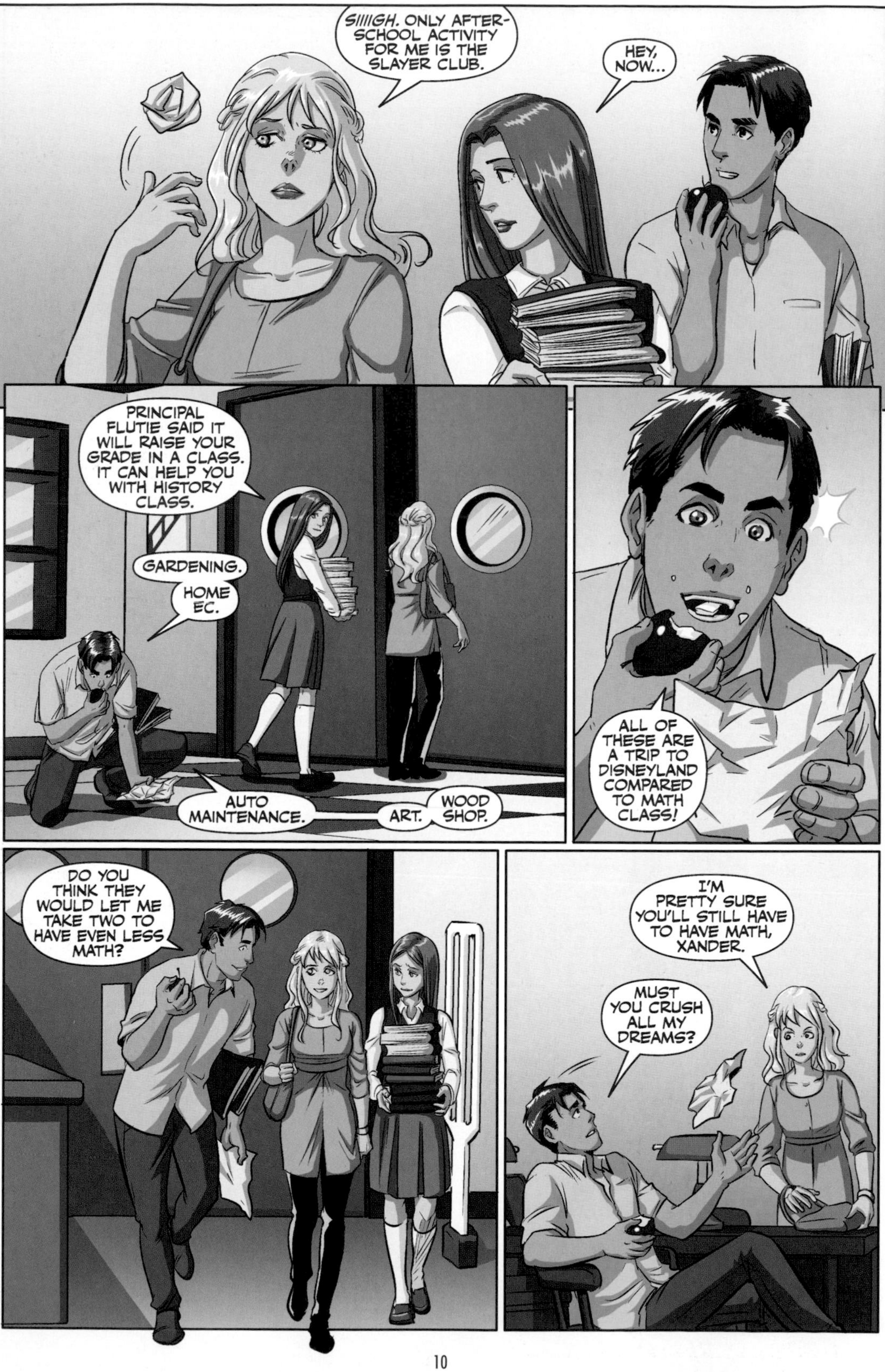
SIIIGH. ONLY AFTER-SCHOOL ACTIVITY FOR ME IS THE SLAYER CLUB.
HEY, NOW...
PRINCIPAL FLUTIE SAID IT WILL RAISE YOUR GRADE IN A CLASS. IT CAN HELP YOU WITH HISTORY CLASS.
GARDENING.
HOME EC.
AUTO MAINTENANCE.
ART.
WOOD SHOP.
ALL OF THESE ARE A TRIP TO DISNEYLAND COMPARED TO MATH CLASS!
DO YOU THINK THEY WOULD LET ME TAKE TWO TO HAVE EVEN LESS MATH?
I'M PRETTY SURE YOU'LL STILL HAVE TO HAVE MATH, XANDER.
MUST YOU CRUSH ALL MY DREAMS?

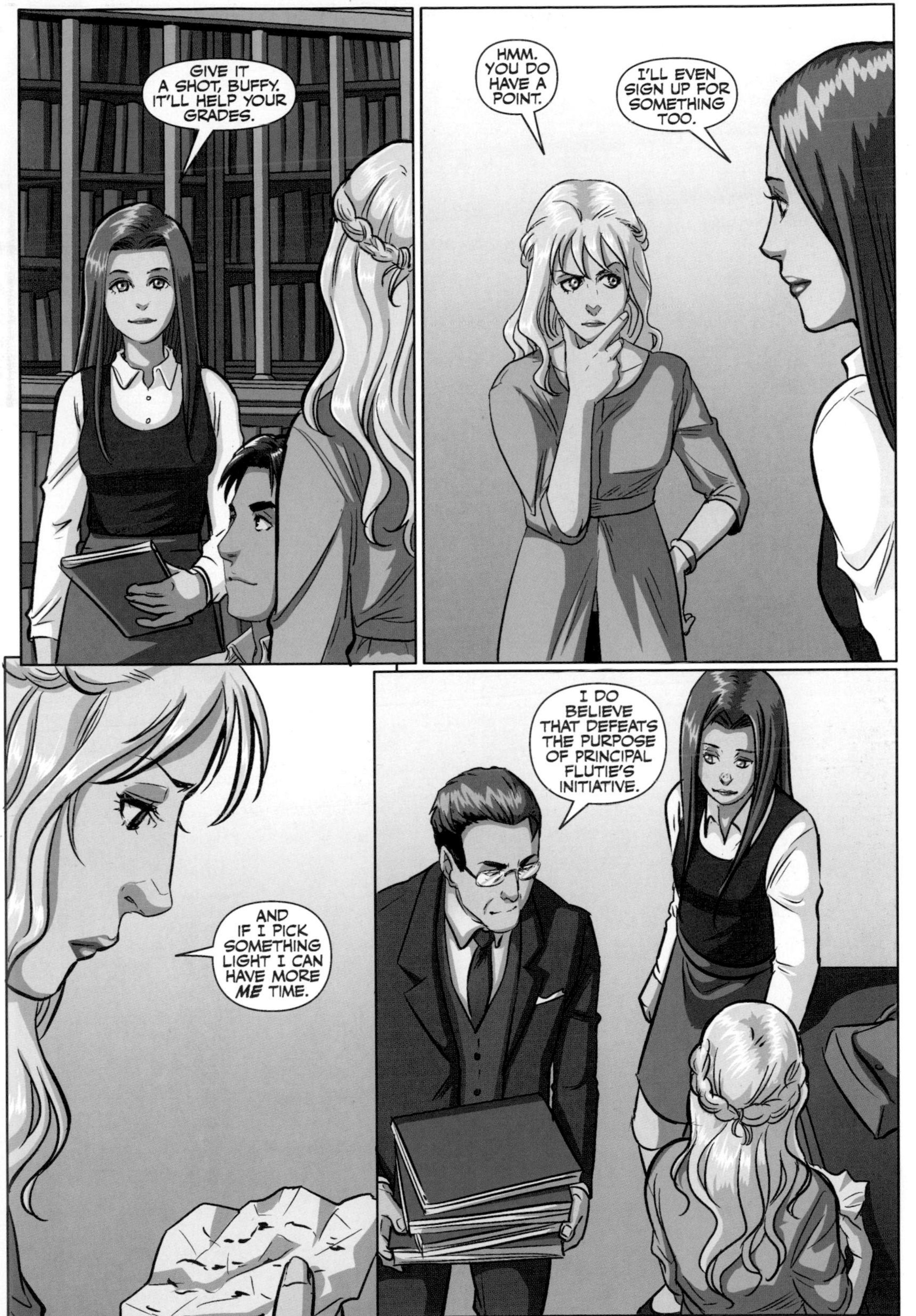
GIVE IT A SHOT, BUFFY. IT'LL HELP YOUR GRADES.
HMM. YOU DO HAVE A POINT.
I'LL EVEN SIGN UP FOR SOMETHING TOO.
AND IF I PICK SOMETHING LIGHT I CAN HAVE MORE *ME* TIME.
I DO BELIEVE THAT DEFEATS THE PURPOSE OF PRINCIPAL FLUTIE'S INITIATIVE.

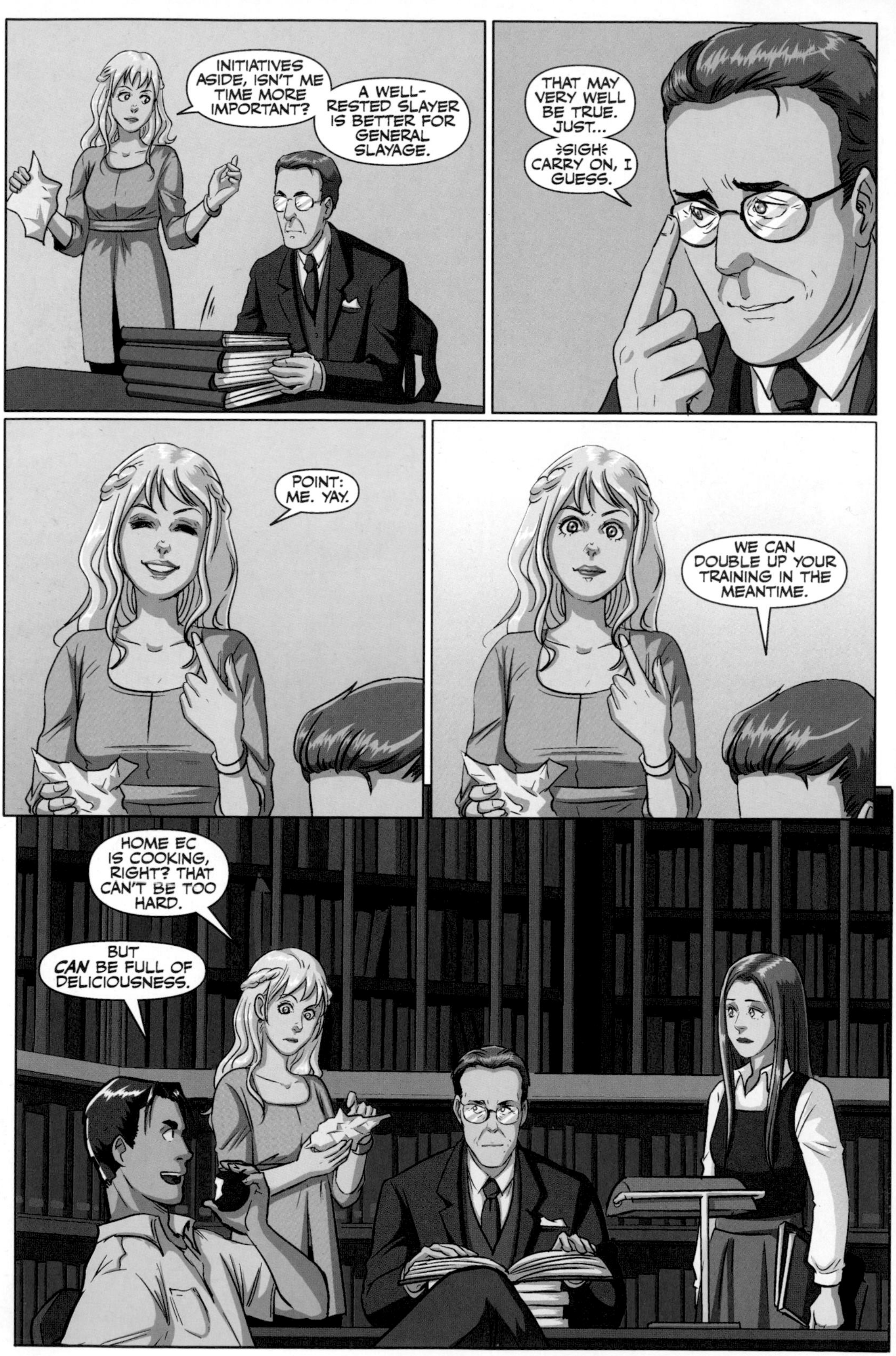
INITIATIVES ASIDE, ISN'T ME TIME MORE IMPORTANT?
A WELL-RESTED SLAYER IS BETTER FOR GENERAL SLAYAGE.
THAT MAY VERY WELL BE TRUE. JUST...
SIGH CARRY ON, I GUESS.
POINT: ME. YAY.
WE CAN DOUBLE UP YOUR TRAINING IN THE MEANTIME.
HOME EC IS COOKING, RIGHT? THAT CAN'T BE TOO HARD.
BUT CAN BE FULL OF DELICIOUSNESS.

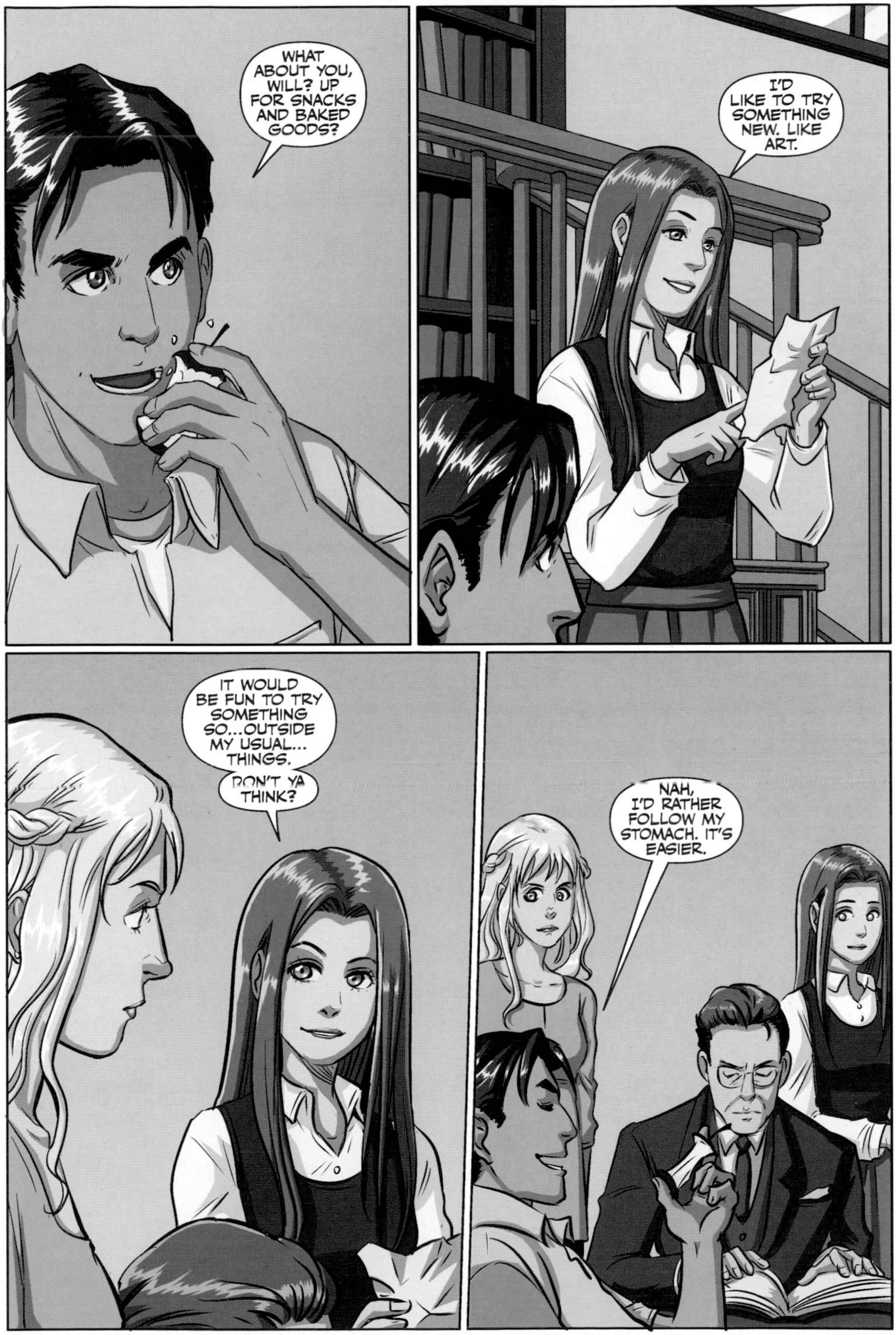
WHAT ABOUT YOU, WILL? UP FOR SNACKS AND BAKED GOODS?
I'D LIKE TO TRY SOMETHING NEW. LIKE ART.
IT WOULD BE FUN TO TRY SOMETHING SO...OUTSIDE MY USUAL... THINGS.
DON'T YA THINK?
NAH, I'D RATHER FOLLOW MY STOMACH. IT'S EASIER.

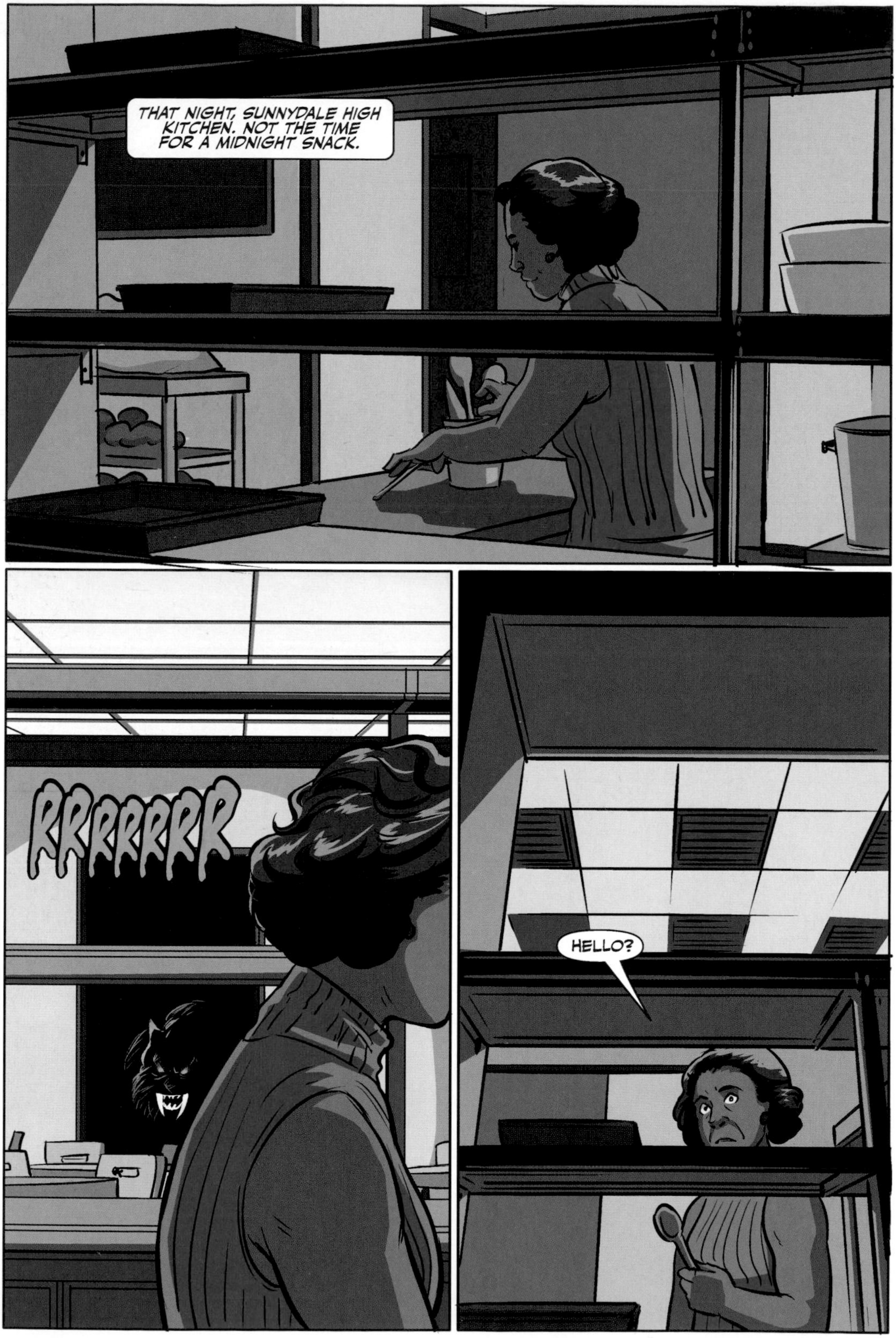
THAT NIGHT, SUNNYDALE HIGH KITCHEN. NOT THE TIME FOR A MIDNIGHT SNACK.
RRRRRRR
HELLO?

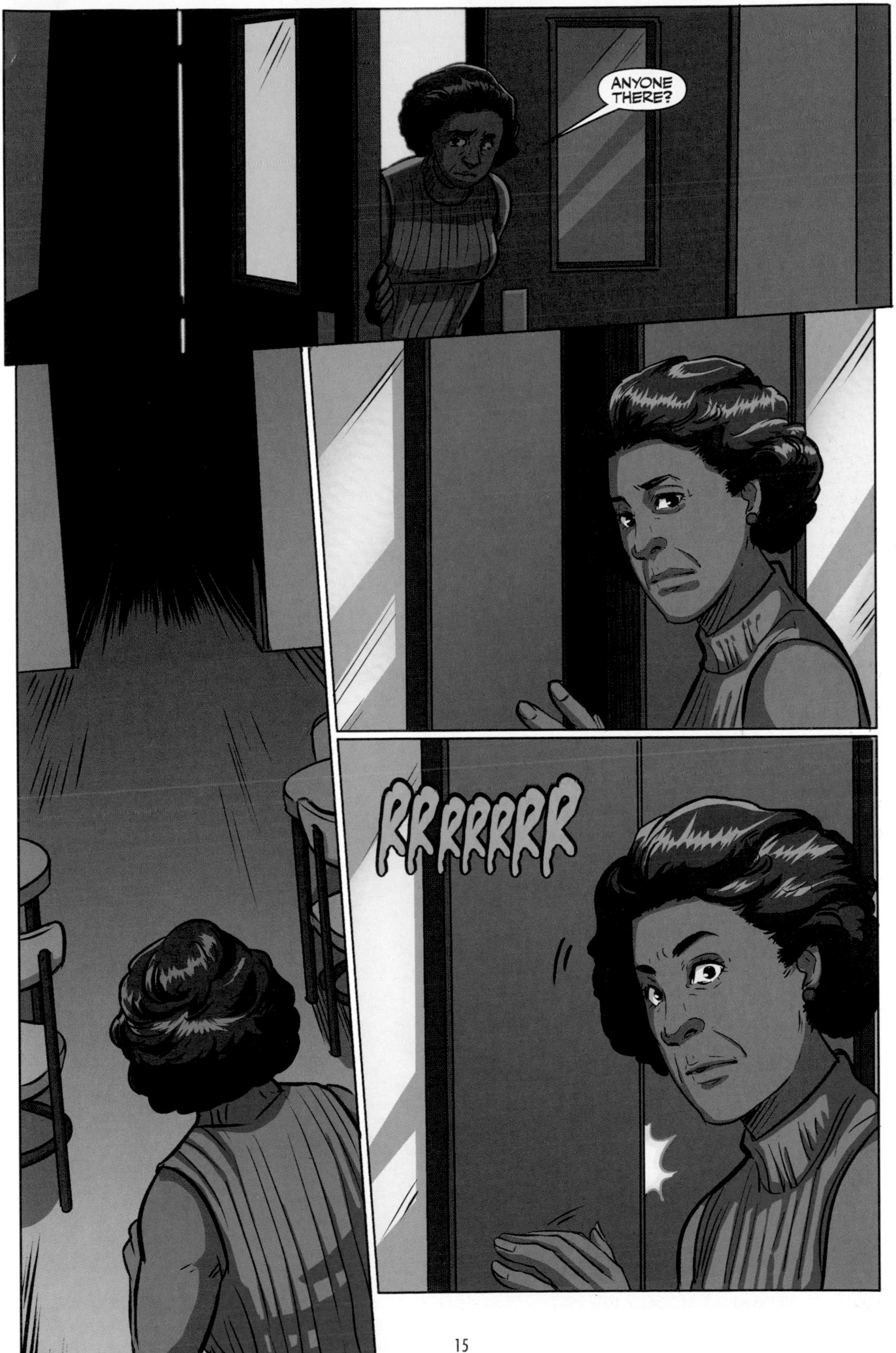
ANYONE THERE?
RRRRRRR

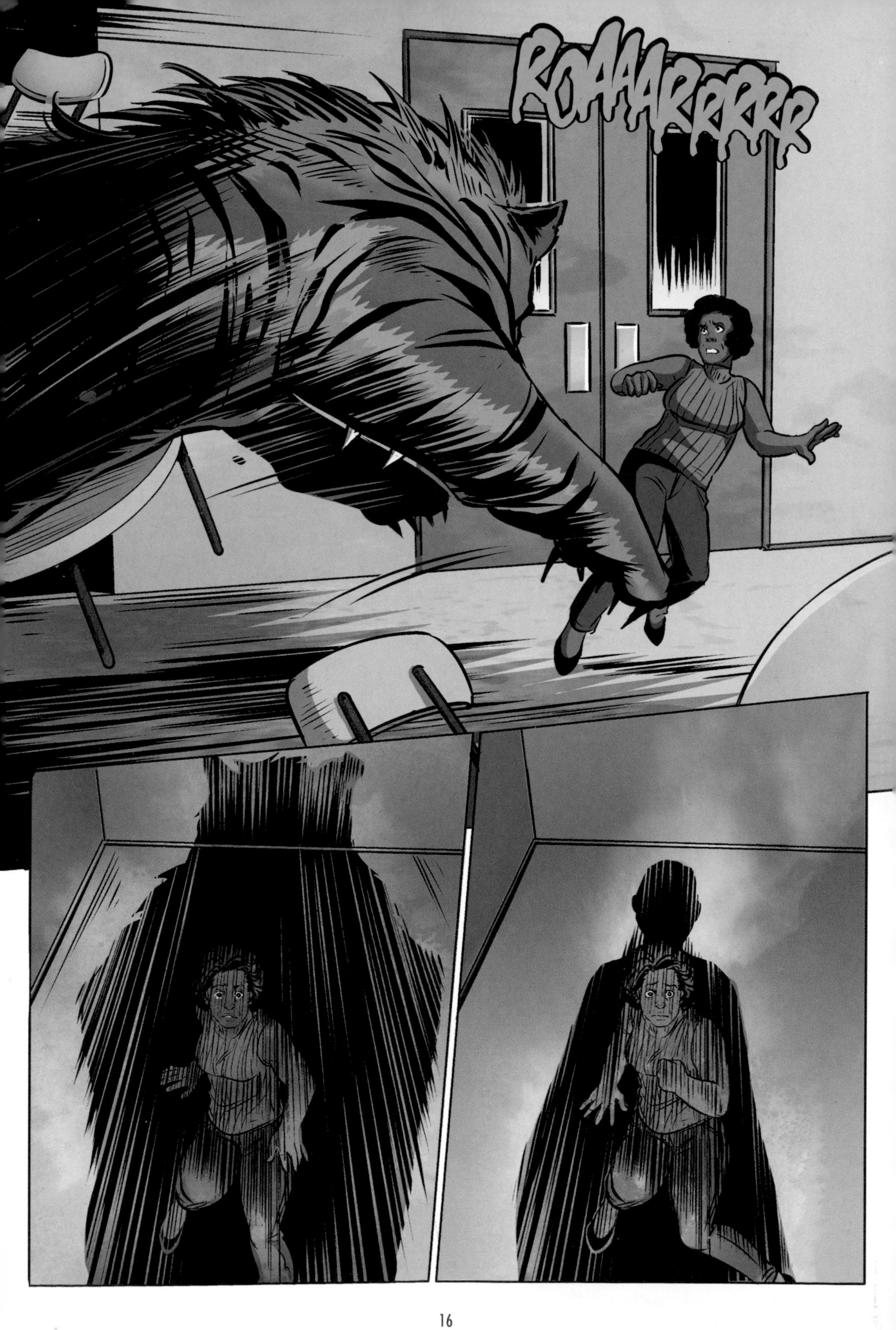
ROAAARRRRR

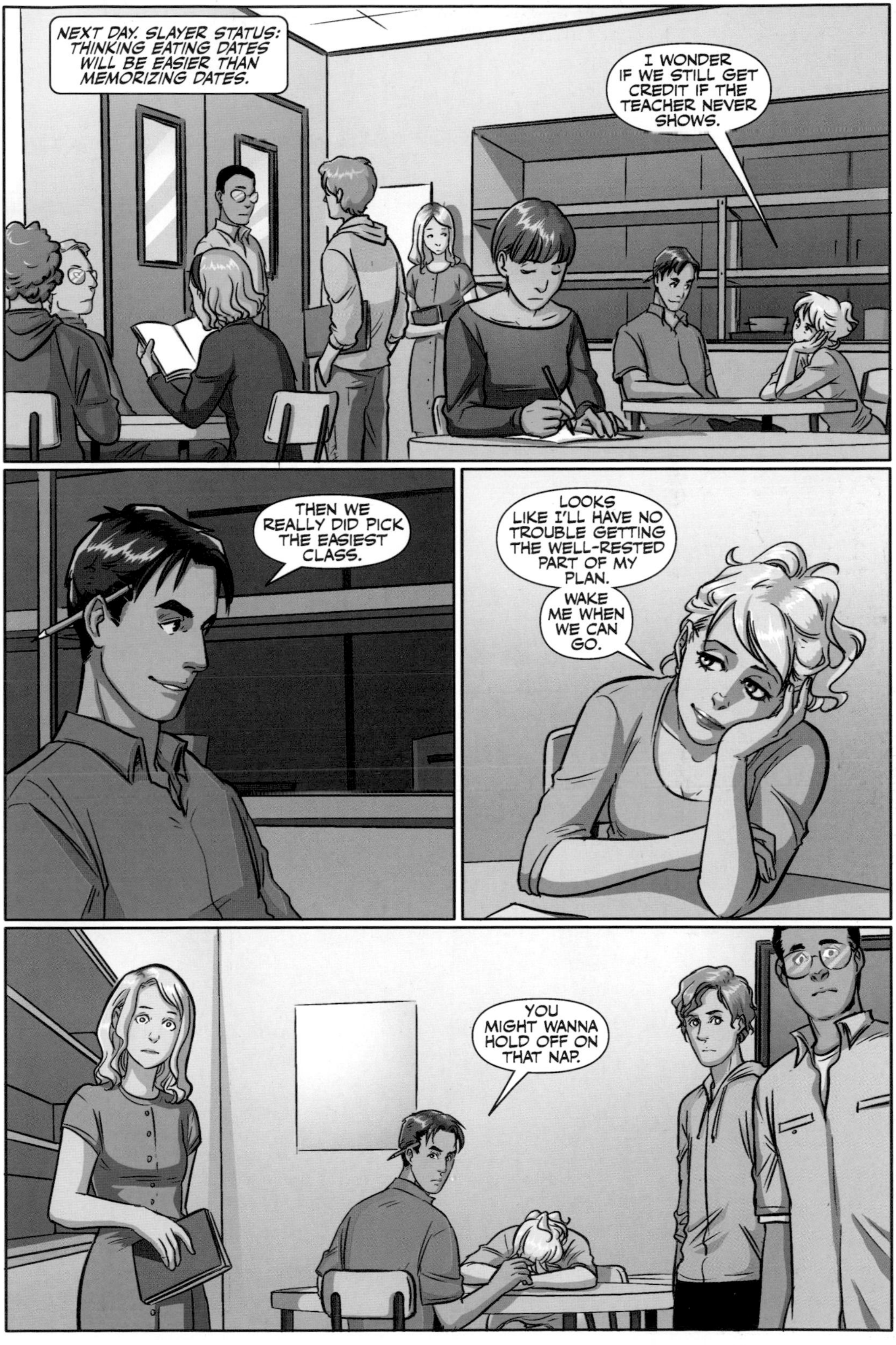
NEXT DAY. SLAYER STATUS: THINKING EATING DATES WILL BE EASIER THAN MEMORIZING DATES.
I WONDER IF WE STILL GET CREDIT IF THE TEACHER NEVER SHOWS.
THEN WE REALLY DID PICK THE EASIEST CLASS.
LOOKS LIKE I'LL HAVE NO TROUBLE GETTING THE WELL-RESTED PART OF MY PLAN.
WAKE ME WHEN WE CAN GO.
YOU MIGHT WANNA HOLD OFF ON THAT NAP.

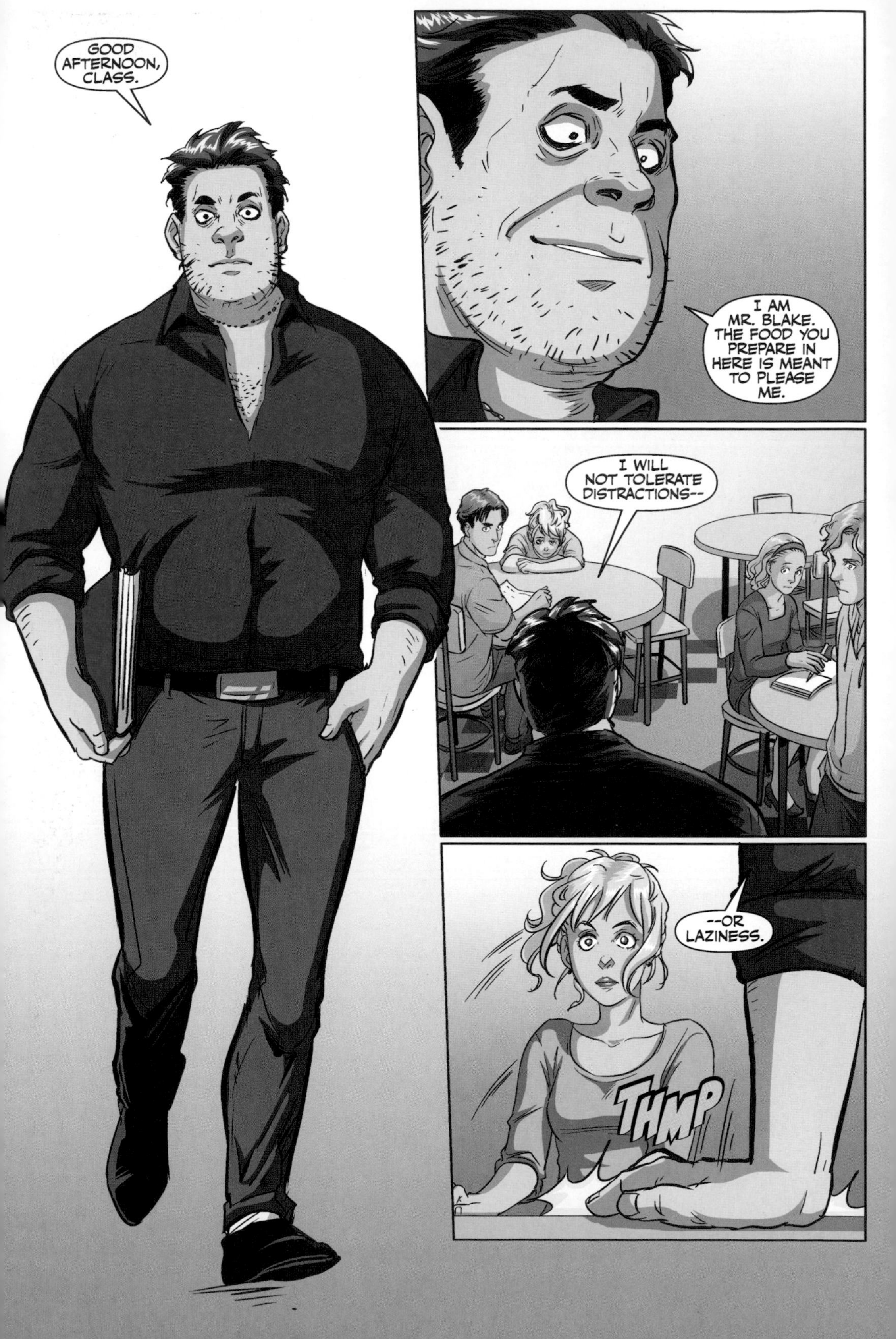
GOOD AFTERNOON, CLASS.
I AM MR. BLAKE. THE FOOD YOU PREPARE IN HERE IS MEANT TO PLEASE ME.
I WILL NOT TOLERATE DISTRACTIONS--
--OR LAZINESS.
THMP

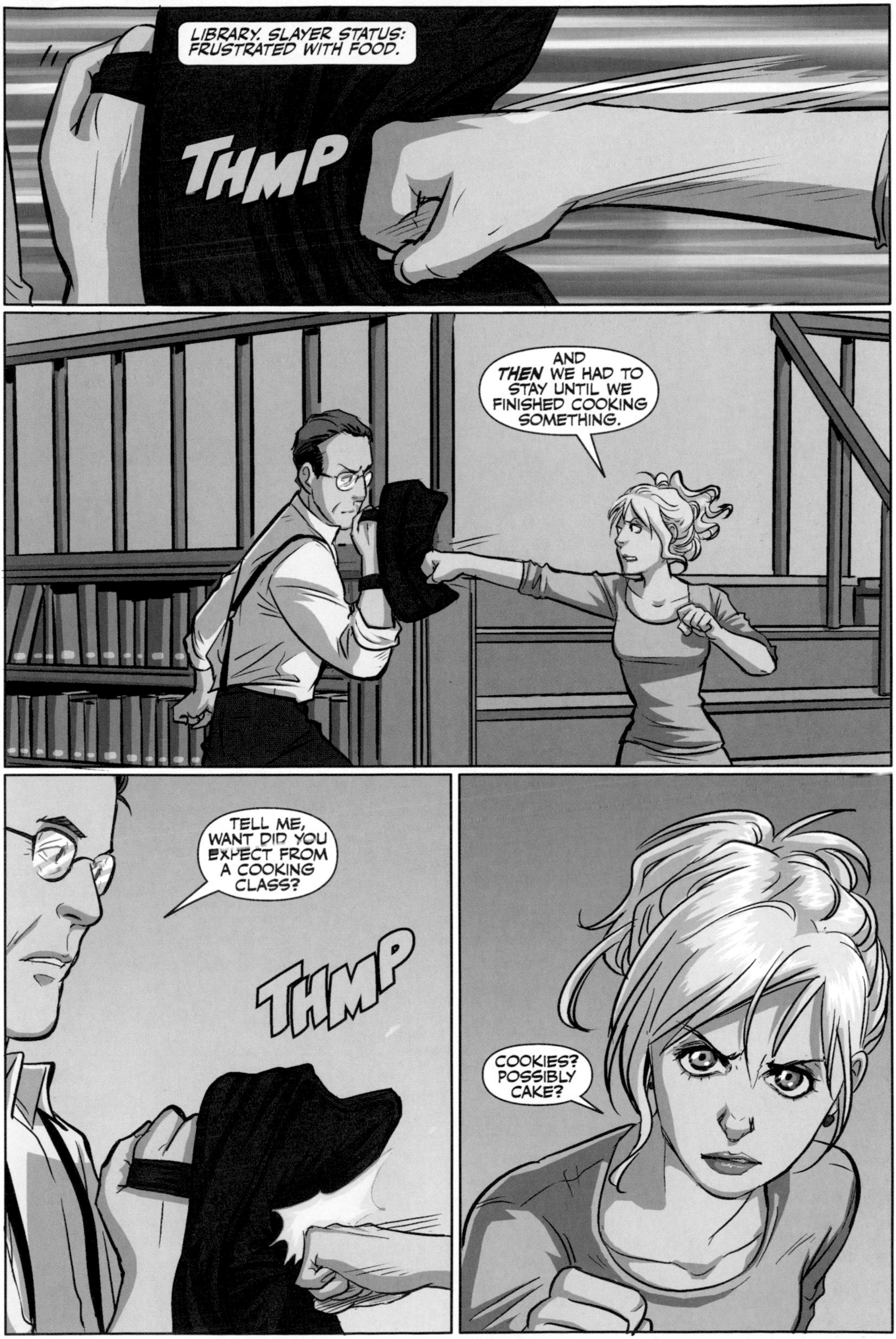
LIBRARY. SLAYER STATUS: FRUSTRATED WITH FOOD.
THMP
AND THEN WE HAD TO STAY UNTIL WE FINISHED COOKING SOMETHING.
TELL ME, WANT DID YOU EXPECT FROM A COOKING CLASS?
THMP
COOKIES? POSSIBLY CAKE?

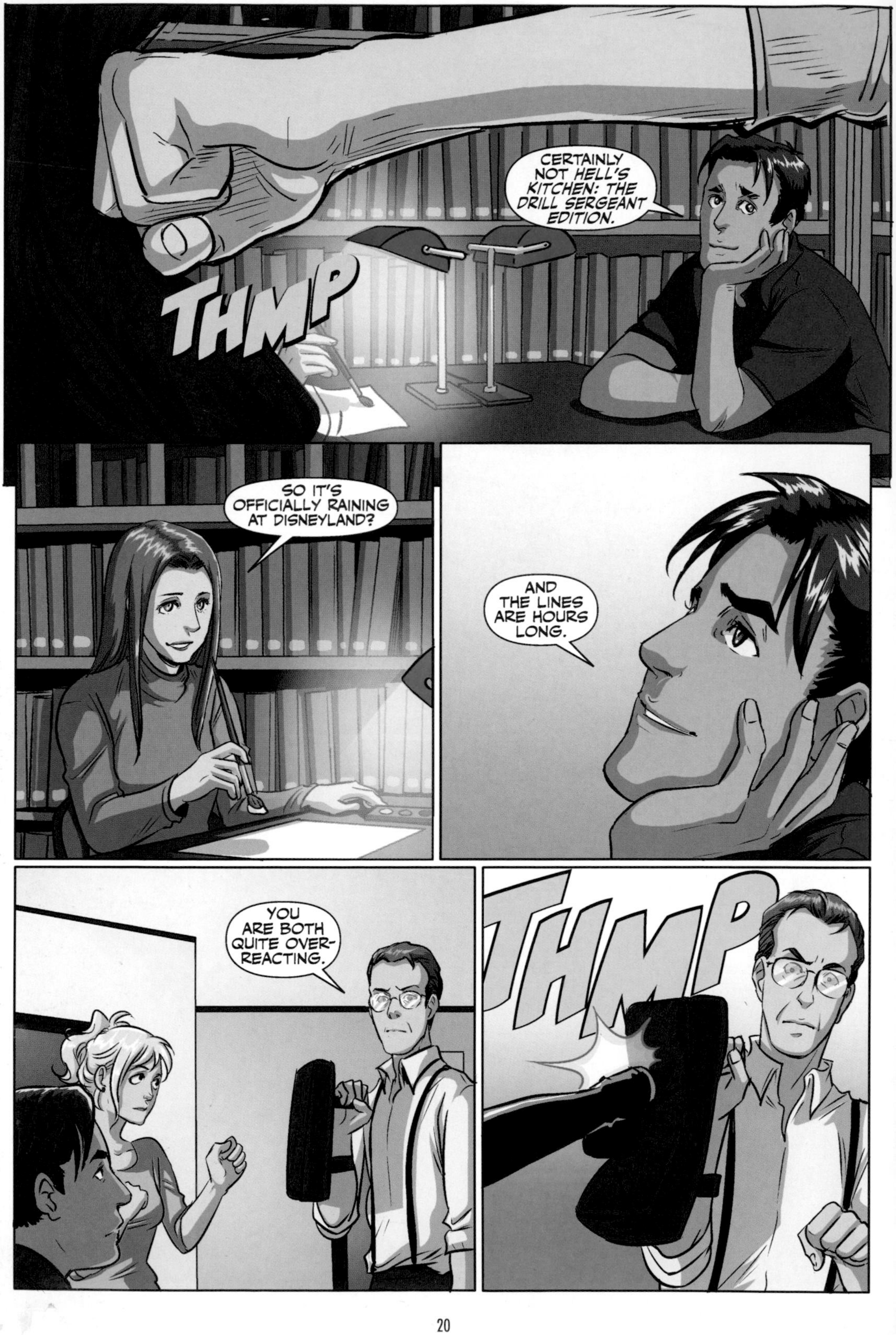
CERTAINLY NOT HELL'S KITCHEN: THE DRILL SERGEANT EDITION.
THMP
SO IT'S OFFICIALLY RAINING AT DISNEYLAND?
AND THE LINES ARE HOURS LONG.
YOU ARE BOTH QUITE OVER-REACTING.
THMP

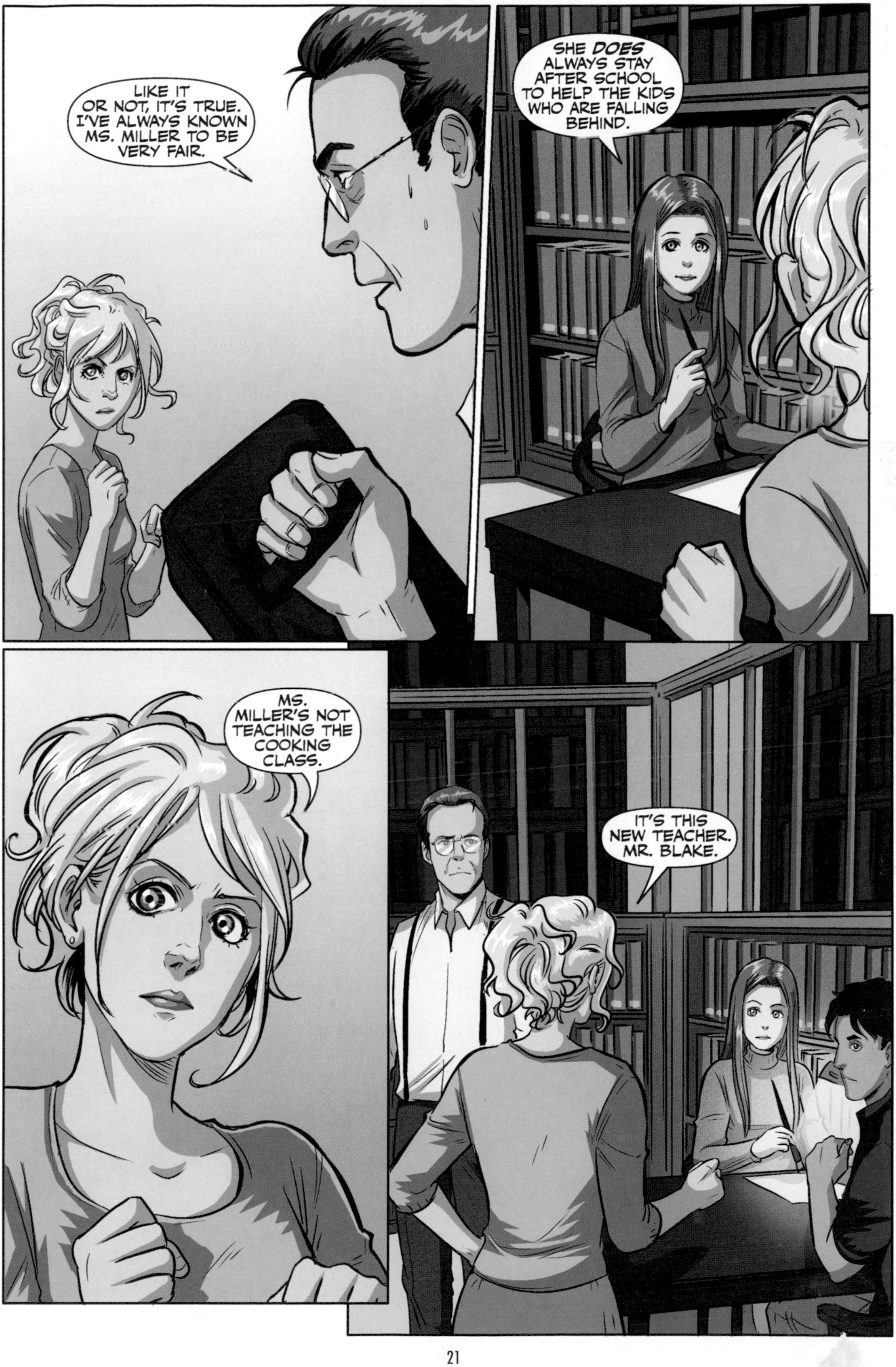
LIKE IT OR NOT, IT'S TRUE. I'VE ALWAYS KNOWN MS. MILLER TO BE VERY FAIR.
SHE DOES ALWAYS STAY AFTER SCHOOL TO HELP THE KIDS WHO ARE FALLING BEHIND.
MS. MILLER'S NOT TEACHING THE COOKING CLASS.
IT'S THIS NEW TEACHER. MR. BLAKE.

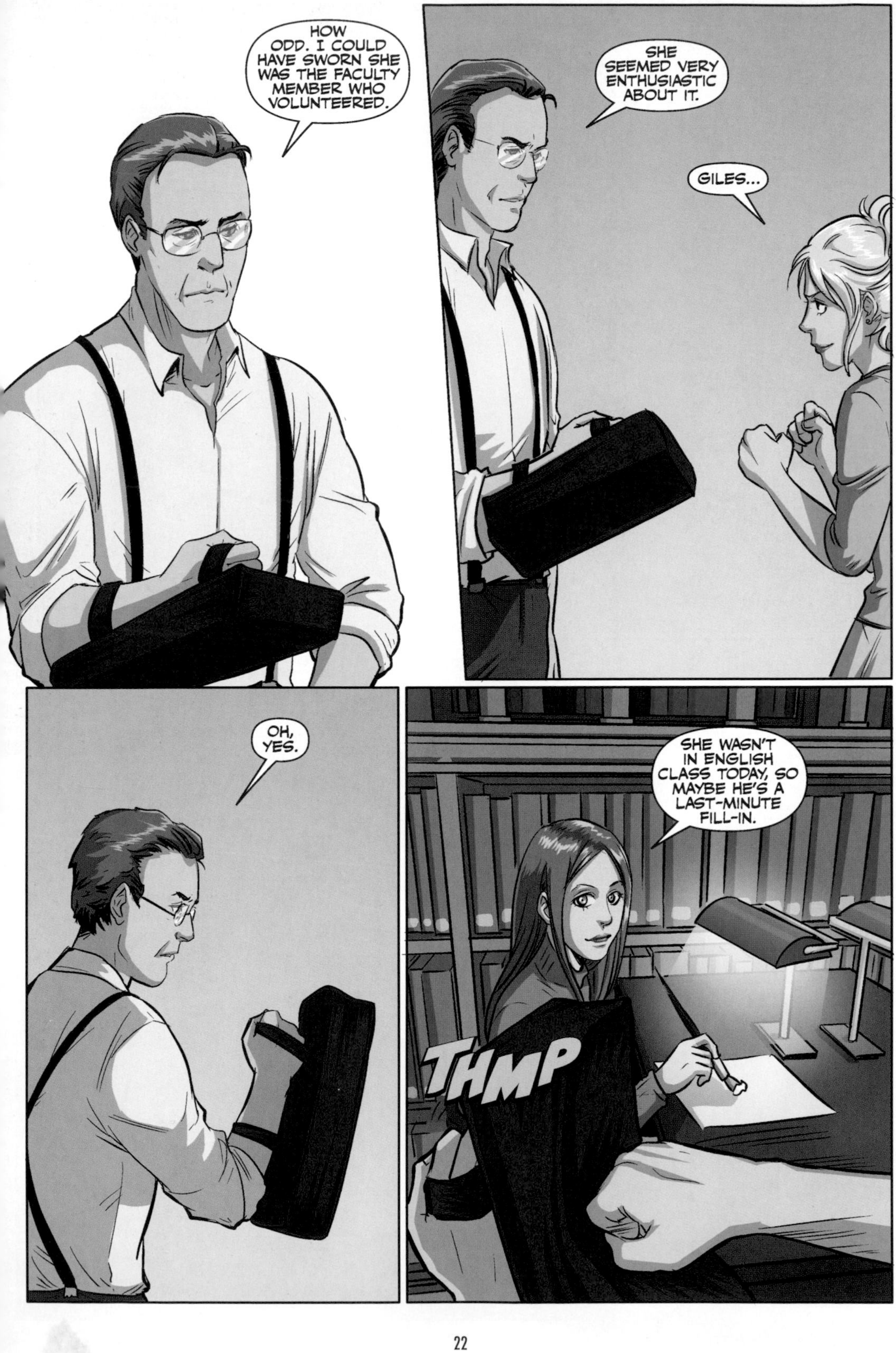
HOW ODD. I COULD HAVE SWORN SHE WAS THE FACULTY MEMBER WHO VOLUNTEERED.
SHE SEEMED VERY ENTHUSIASTIC ABOUT IT.
GILES...
OH, YES.
SHE WASN'T IN ENGLISH CLASS TODAY, SO MAYBE HE'S A LAST-MINUTE FILL-IN.
THMP

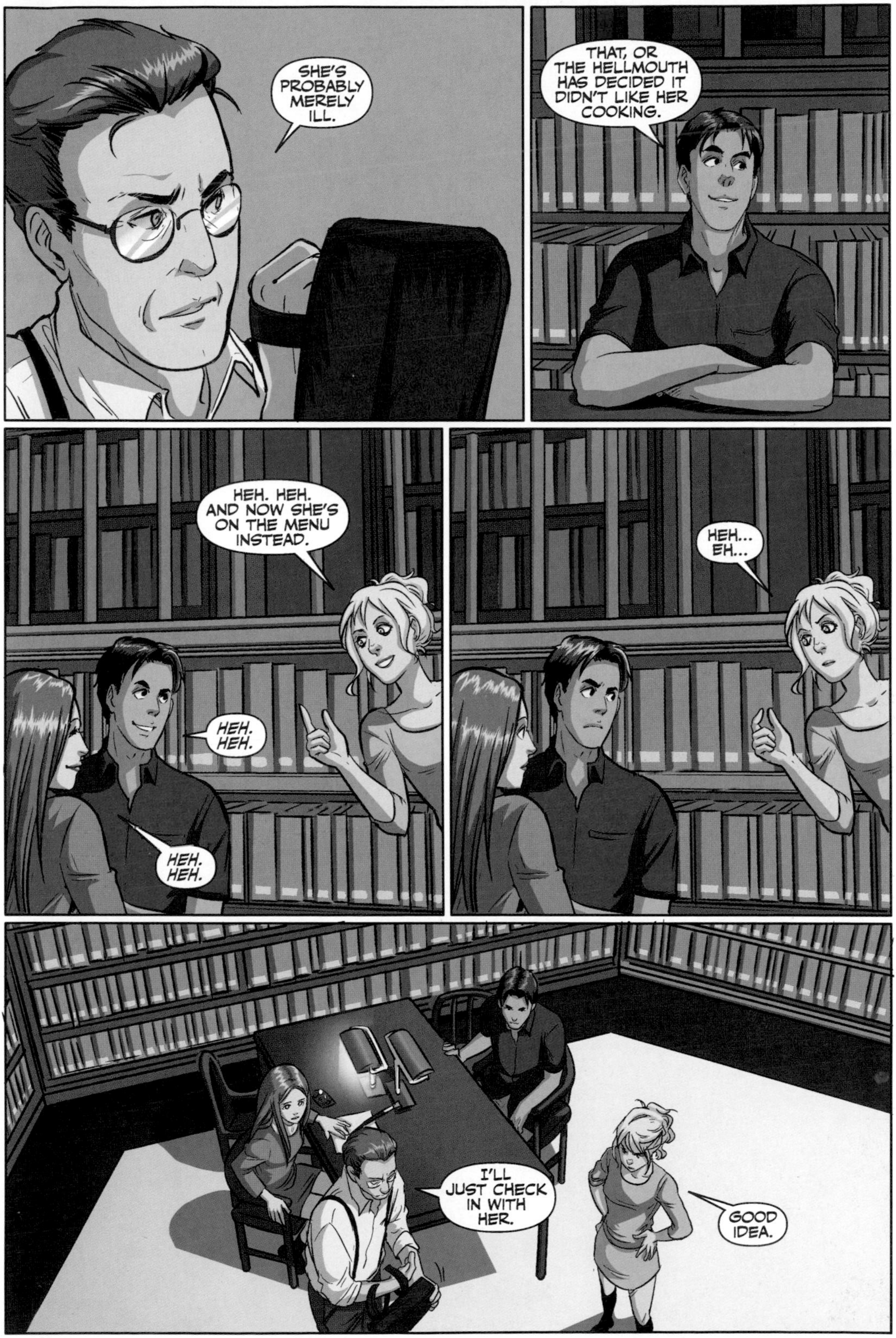
SHE'S PROBABLY MERELY ILL.
THAT, OR THE HELLMOUTH HAS DECIDED IT DIDN'T LIKE HER COOKING.
HEH. HEH. AND NOW SHE'S ON THE MENU INSTEAD.
HEH. HEH.
HEH. HEH.
HEH... EH...
I'LL JUST CHECK IN WITH HER.
GOOD IDEA.

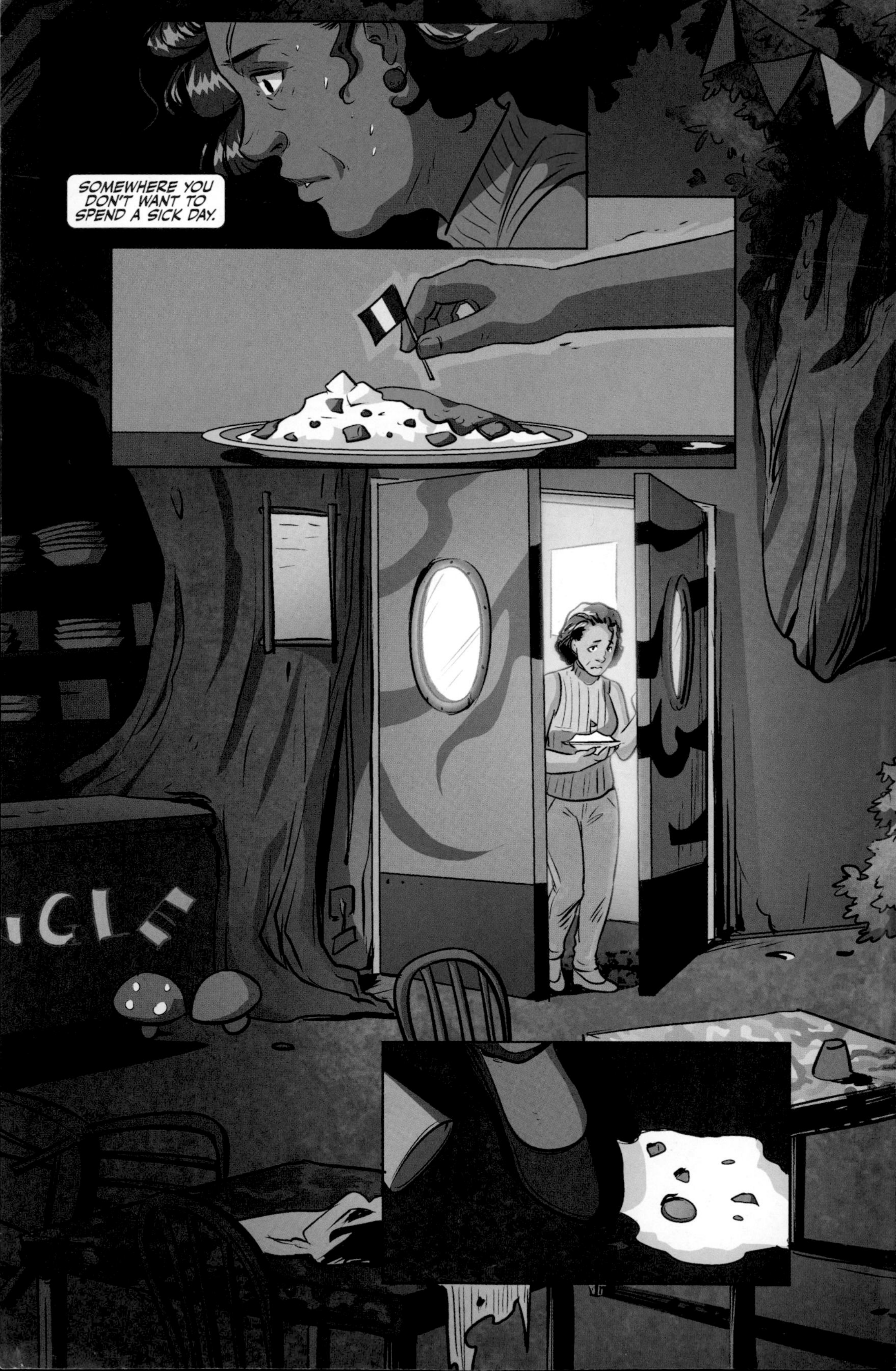
SOMEWHERE YOU DON'T WANT TO SPEND A SICK DAY.

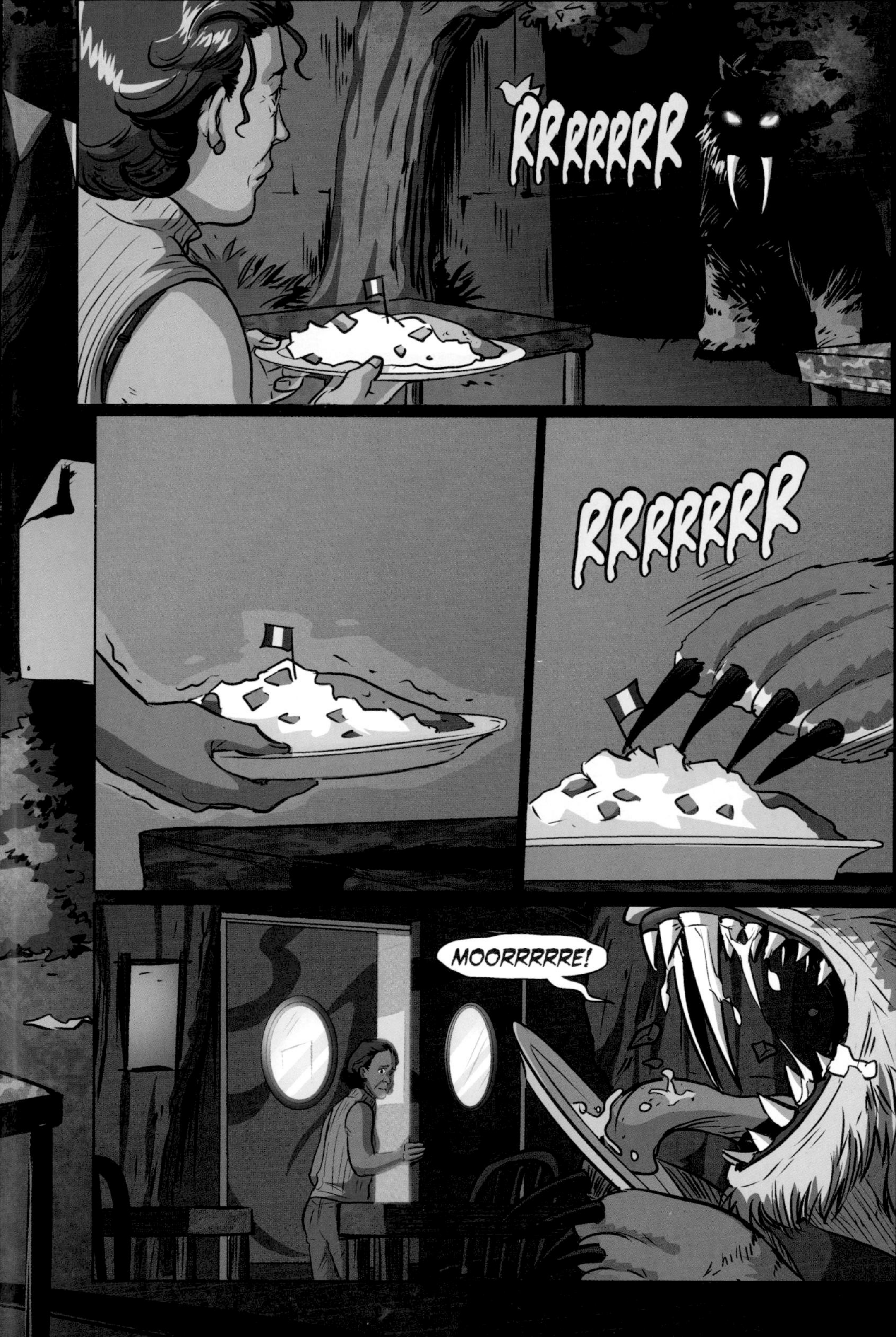
RRRRRRR
RRRRRRR
MOORRRRRE!

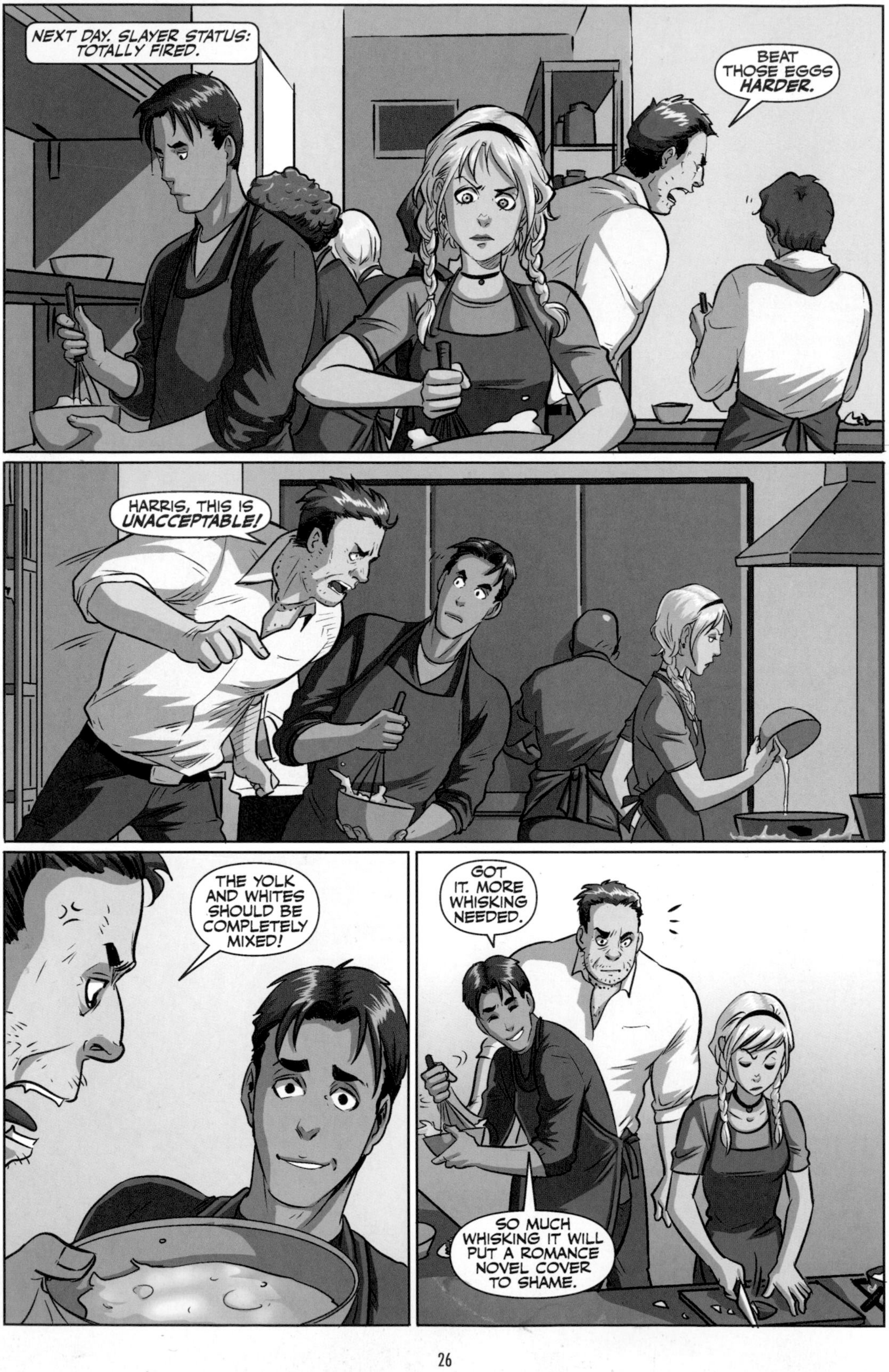
NEXT DAY. SLAYER STATUS: TOTALLY FIRED.
BEAT THOSE EGGS HARDER.
HARRIS, THIS IS UNACCEPTABLE!
THE YOLK AND WHITES SHOULD BE COMPLETELY MIXED!
GOT IT. MORE WHISKING NEEDED.
SO MUCH WHISKING IT WILL PUT A ROMANCE NOVEL COVER TO SHAME.

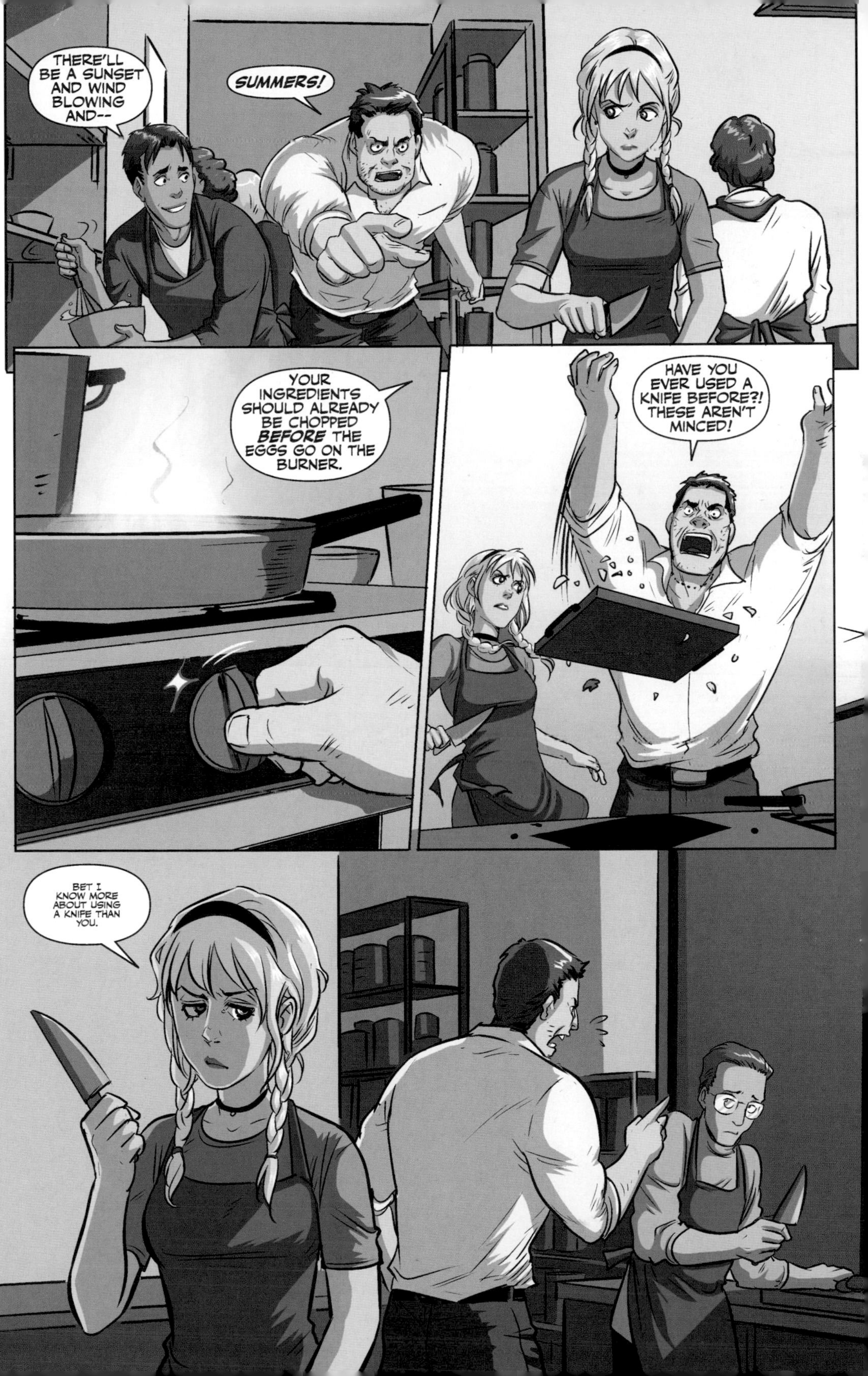
THERE'LL BE A SUNSET AND WIND BLOWING AND--
SUMMERS!
YOUR INGREDIENTS SHOULD ALREADY BE CHOPPED BEFORE THE EGGS GO ON THE BURNER.
HAVE YOU EVER USED A KNIFE BEFORE?! THESE AREN'T MINCED!
BET I KNOW MORE ABOUT USING A KNIFE THAN YOU.

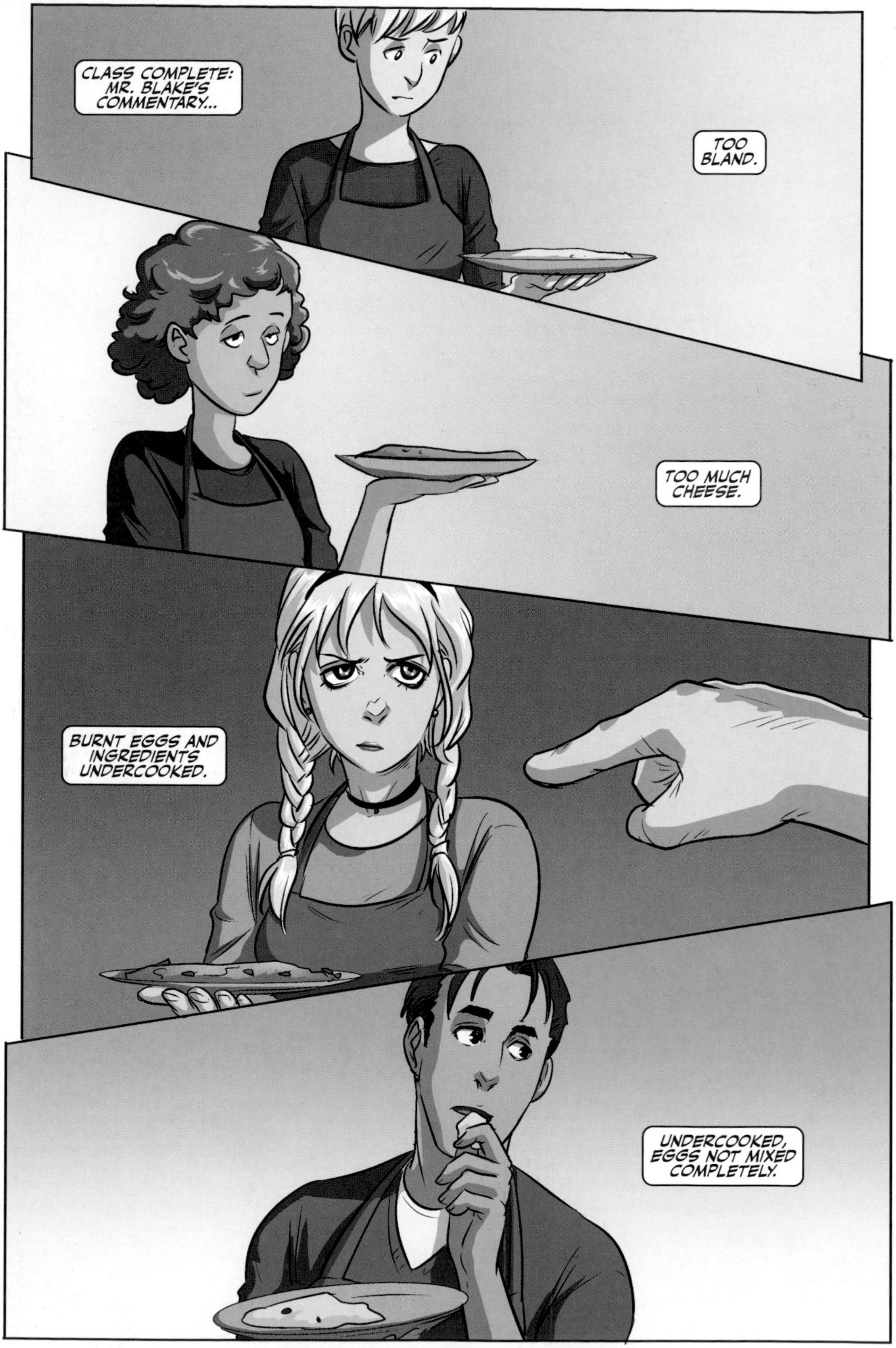
CLASS COMPLETE: MR. BLAKE'S COMMENTARY...
TOO BLAND.
TOO MUCH CHEESE.
BURNT EGGS AND INGREDIENTS UNDERCOOKED.
UNDERCOOKED, EGGS NOT MIXED COMPLETELY.

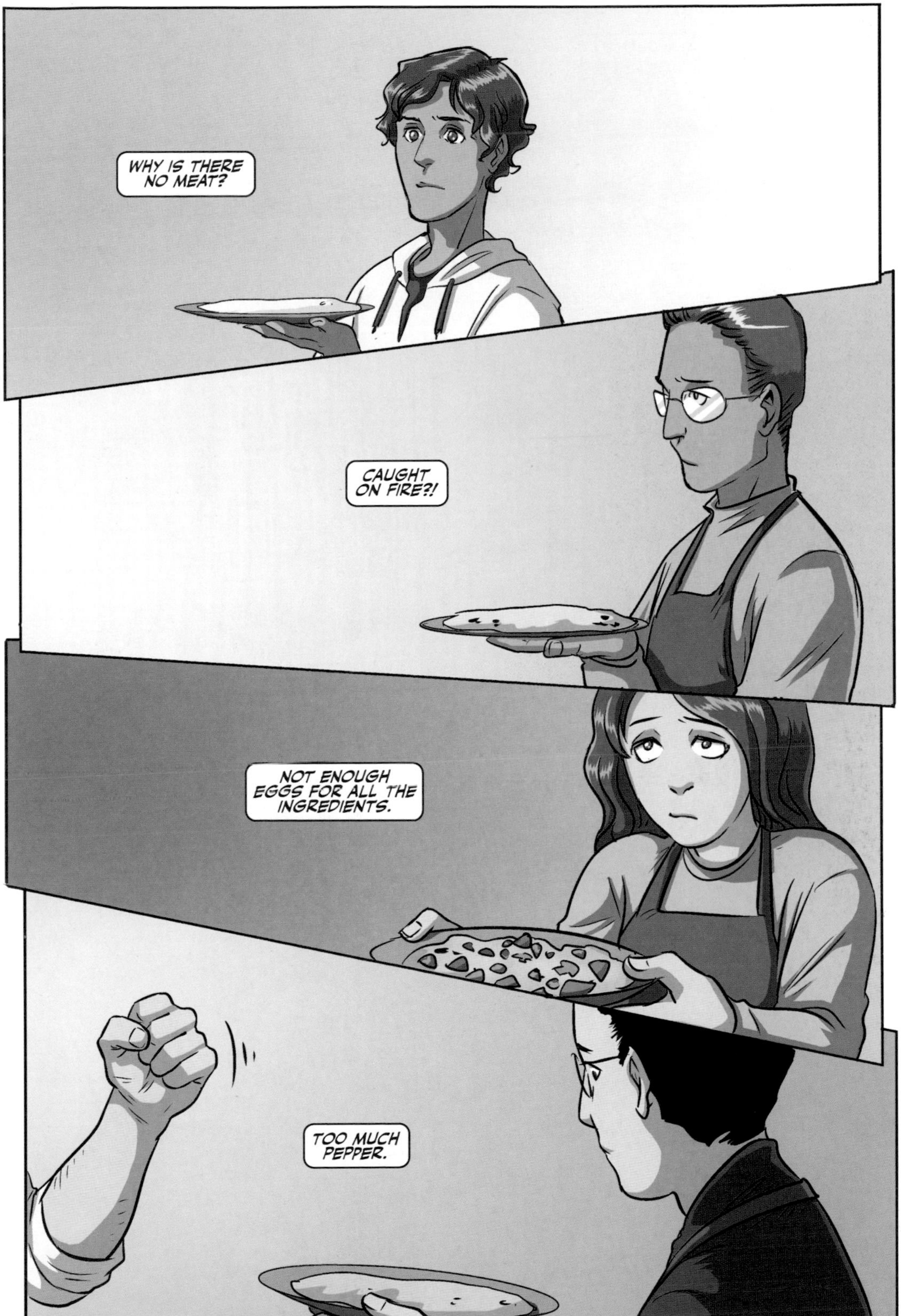
WHY IS THERE NO MEAT?
CAUGHT ON FIRE?!
NOT ENOUGH EGGS FOR ALL THE INGREDIENTS.
TOO MUCH PEPPER.

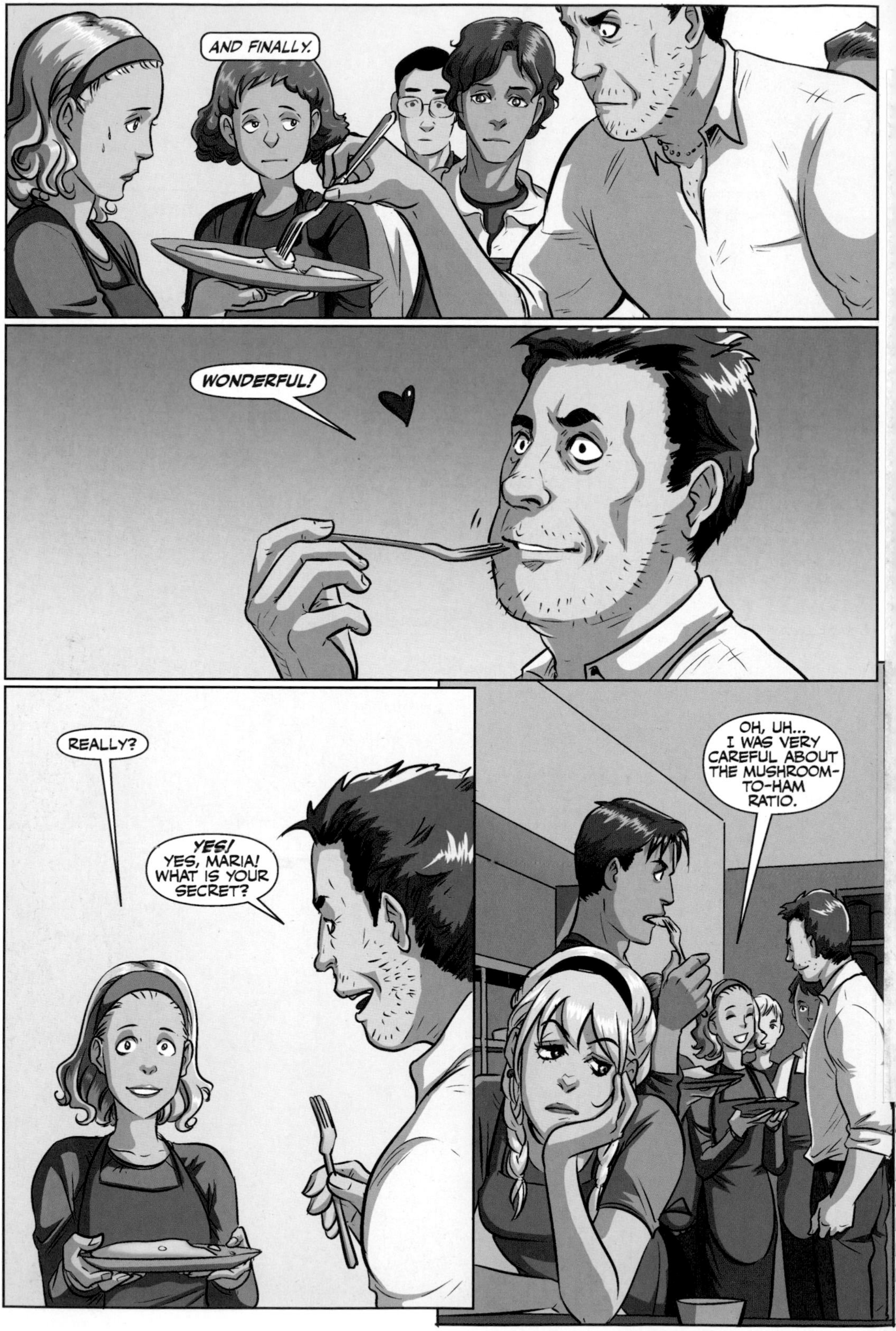
AND FINALLY.
WONDERFUL!
REALLY?
YES! YES, MARIA! WHAT IS YOUR SECRET?
OH, UH... I WAS VERY CAREFUL ABOUT THE MUSHROOM-TO-HAM RATIO.

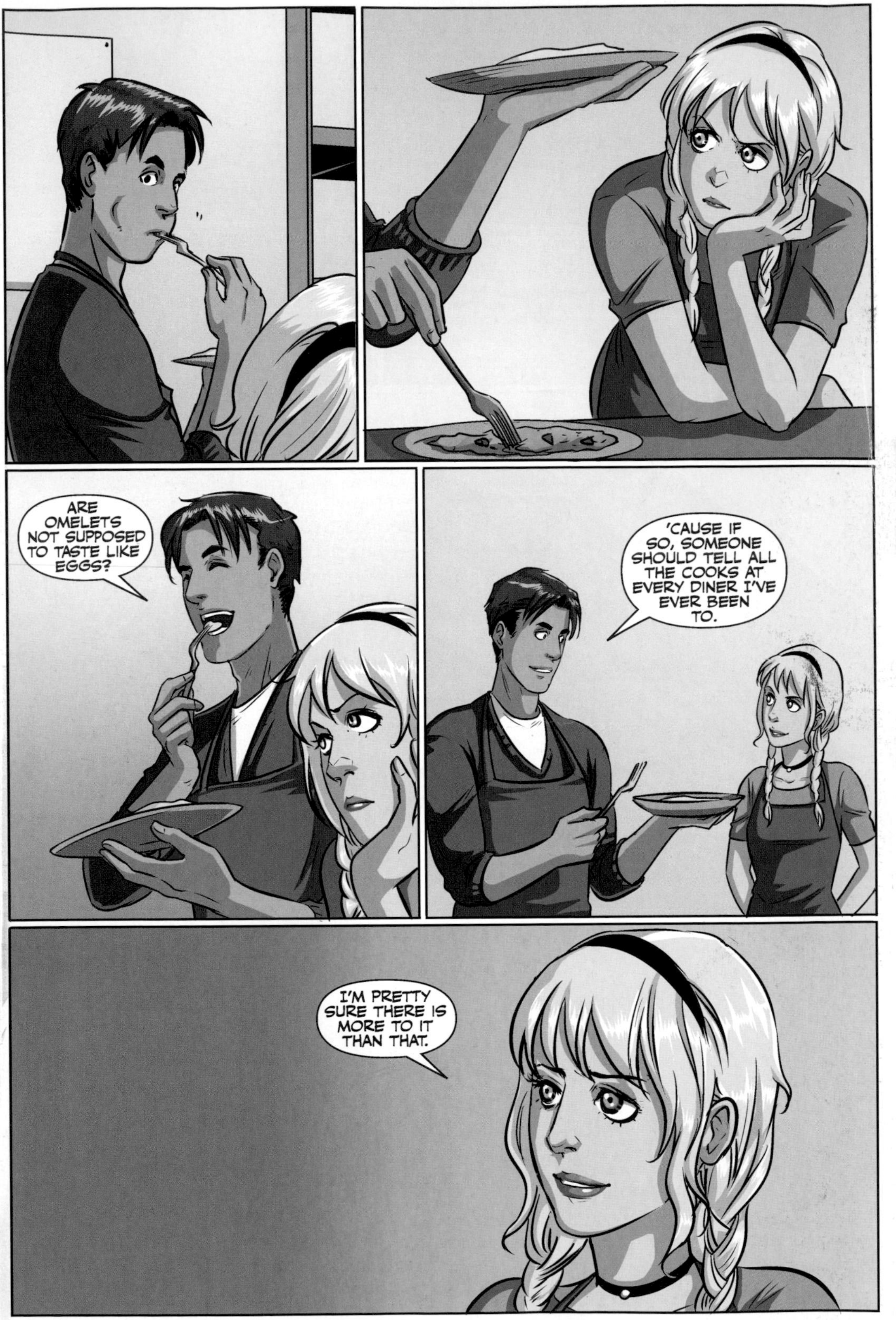
ARE OMELETS NOT SUPPOSED TO TASTE LIKE EGGS?
'CAUSE IF SO, SOMEONE SHOULD TELL ALL THE COOKS AT EVERY DINER I'VE EVER BEEN TO.
I'M PRETTY SURE THERE IS MORE TO IT THAN THAT.

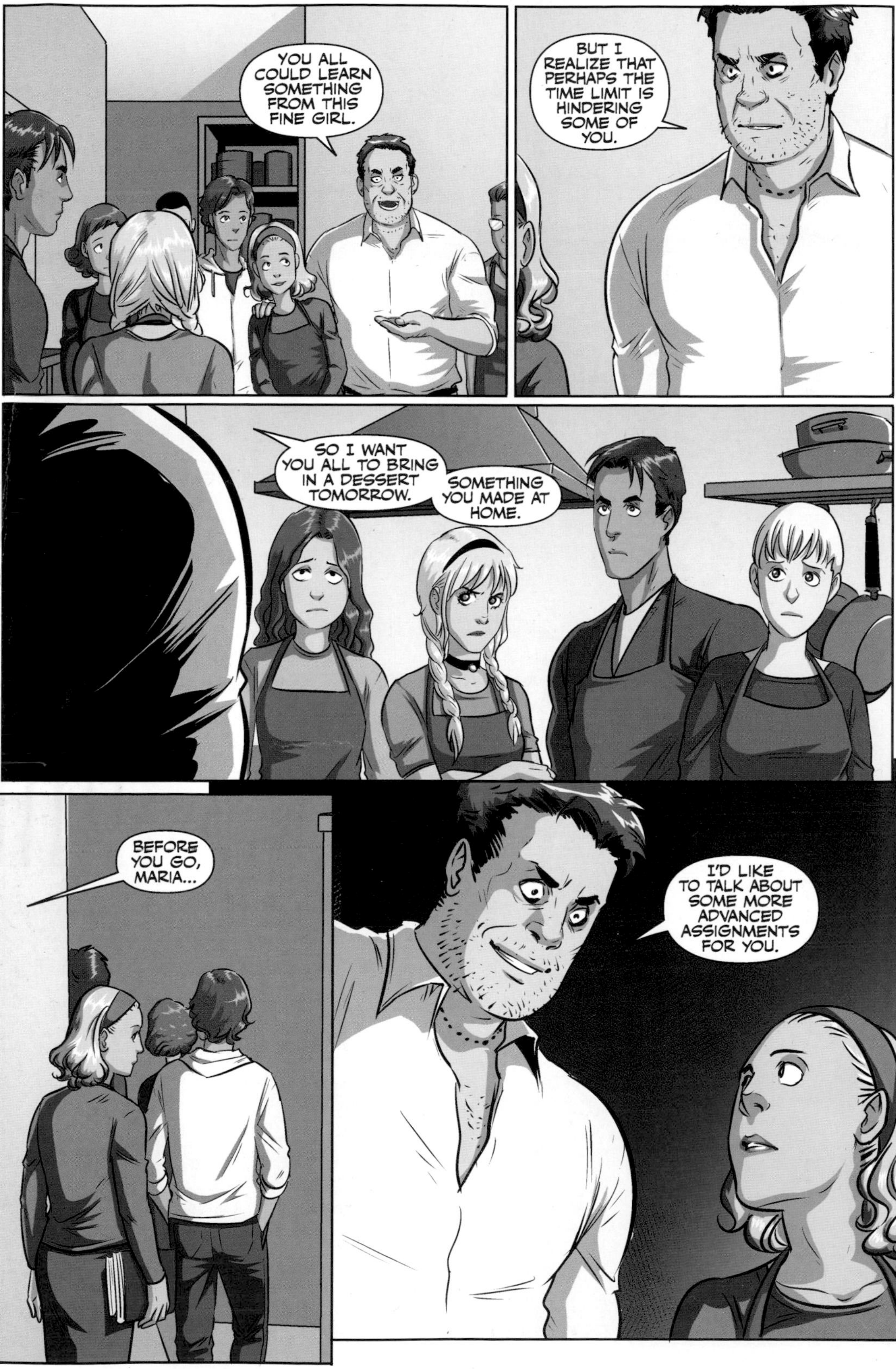
YOU ALL COULD LEARN SOMETHING FROM THIS FINE GIRL.
BUT I REALIZE THAT PERHAPS THE TIME LIMIT IS HINDERING SOME OF YOU.
SO I WANT YOU ALL TO BRING IN A DESSERT TOMORROW.
SOMETHING YOU MADE AT HOME.
BEFORE YOU GO, MARIA...
I'D LIKE TO TALK ABOUT SOME MORE ADVANCED ASSIGNMENTS FOR YOU.

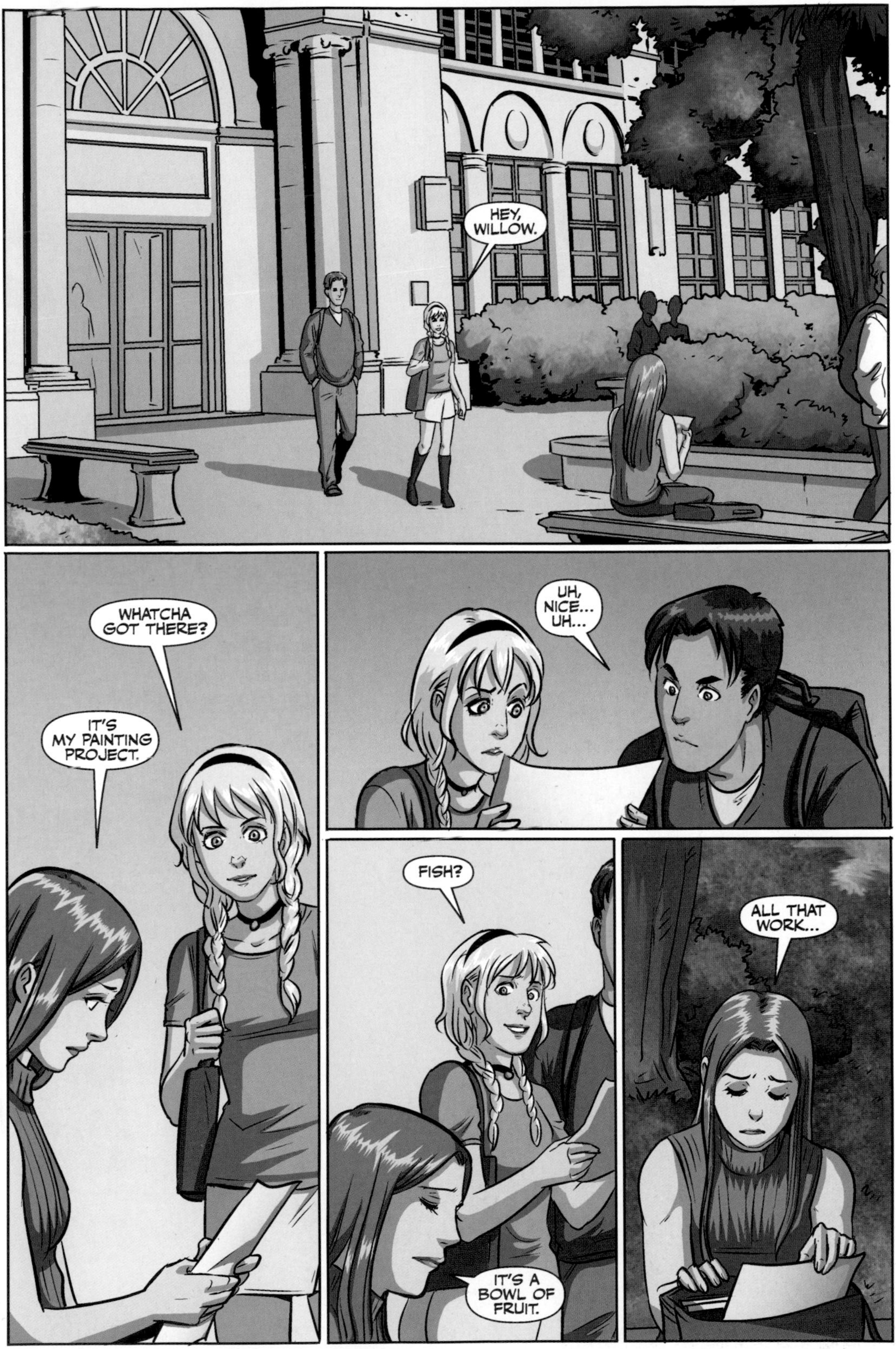
HEY, WILLOW.
WHATCHA GOT THERE?
IT'S MY PAINTING PROJECT.
UH, NICE... UH...
FISH?
IT'S A BOWL OF FRUIT.
ALL THAT WORK...

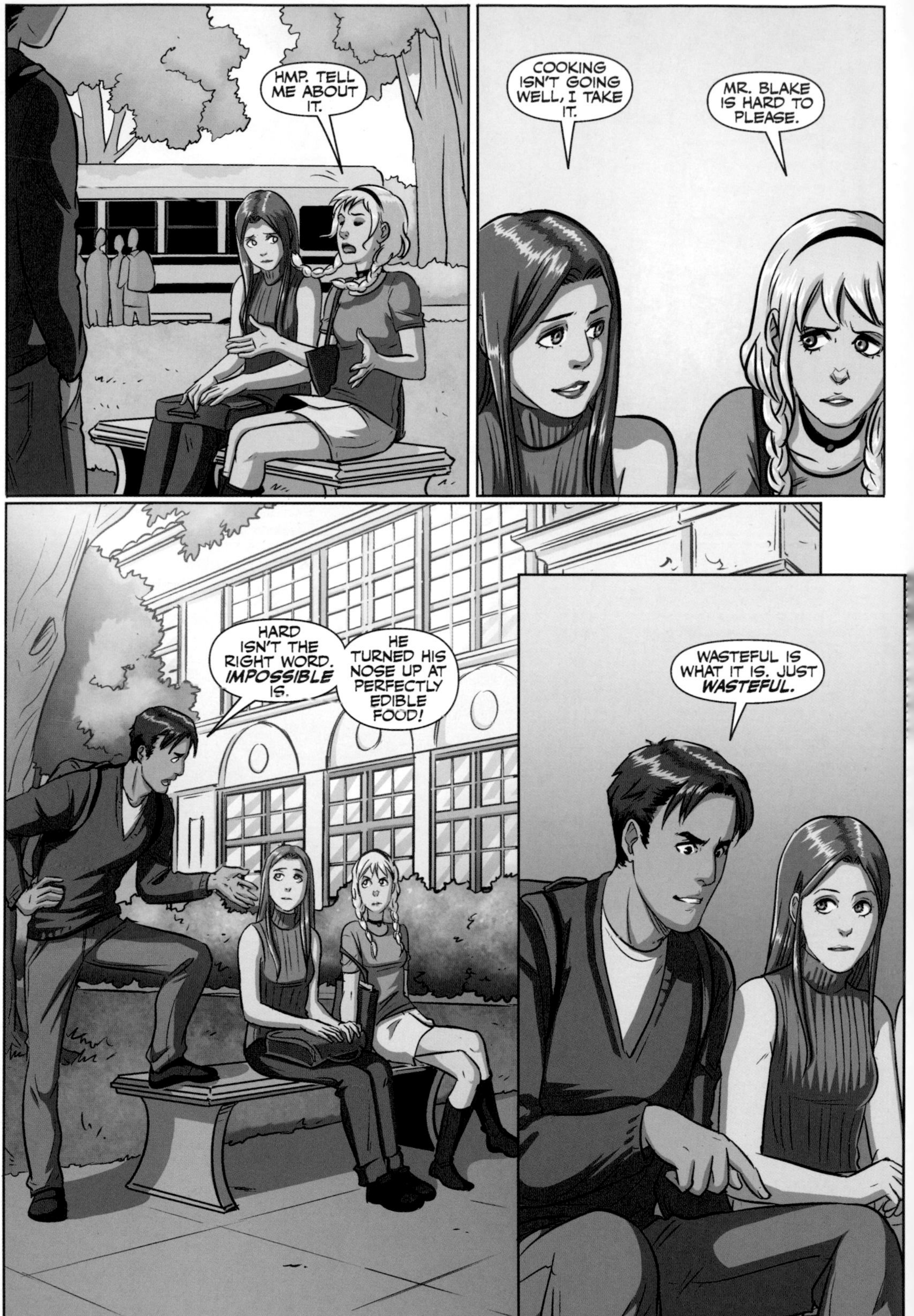
HMP. TELL ME ABOUT IT.
COOKING ISN'T GOING WELL, I TAKE IT.
MR. BLAKE IS HARD TO PLEASE.
HARD ISN'T THE RIGHT WORD. IMPOSSIBLE IS.
HE TURNED HIS NOSE UP AT PERFECTLY EDIBLE FOOD!
WASTEFUL IS WHAT IT IS. JUST WASTEFUL.

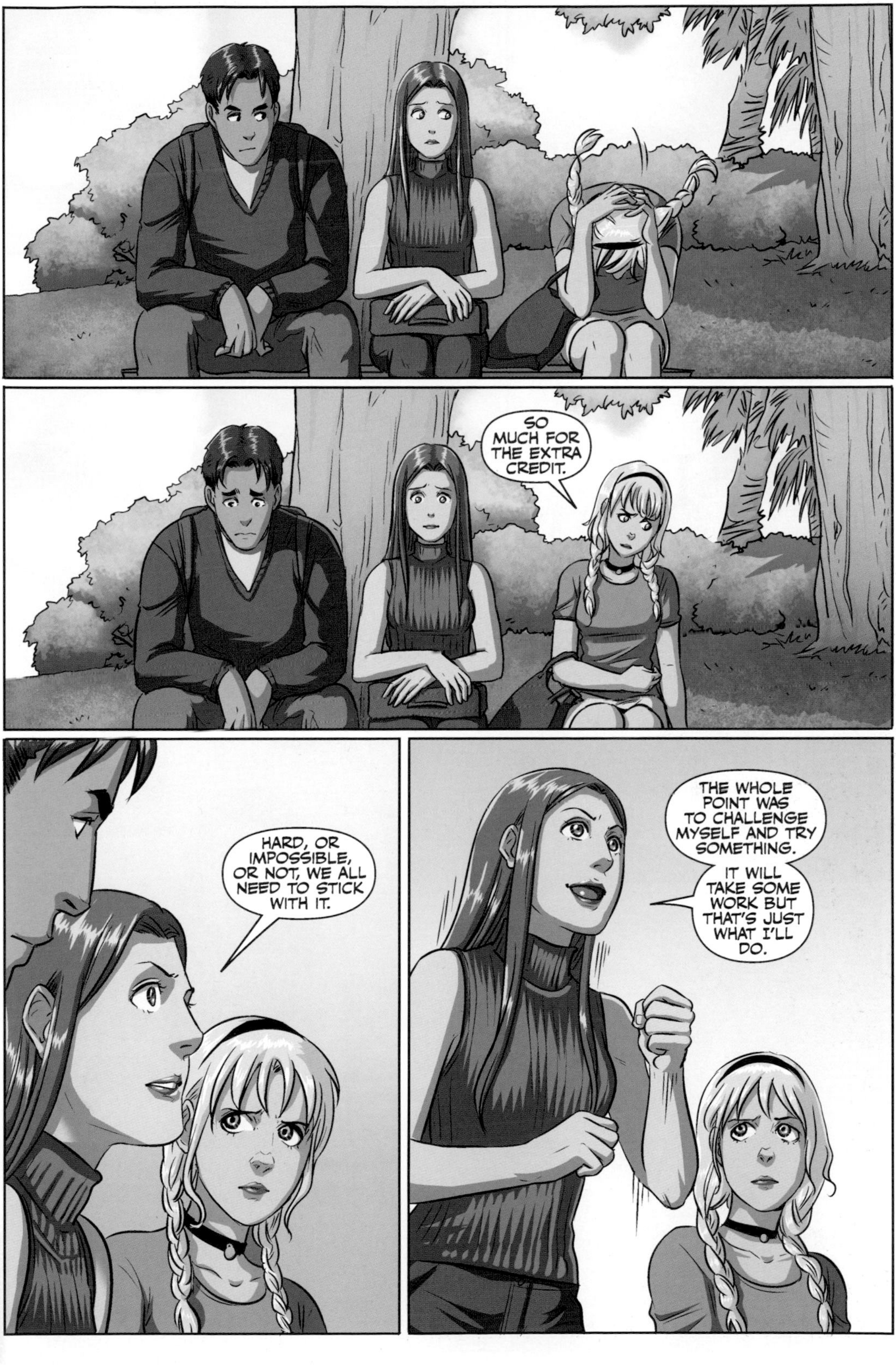
SO MUCH FOR THE EXTRA CREDIT.
HARD, OR IMPOSSIBLE, OR NOT, WE ALL NEED TO STICK WITH IT.
THE WHOLE POINT WAS TO CHALLENGE MYSELF AND TRY SOMETHING.
IT WILL TAKE SOME WORK BUT THAT'S JUST WHAT I'LL DO.

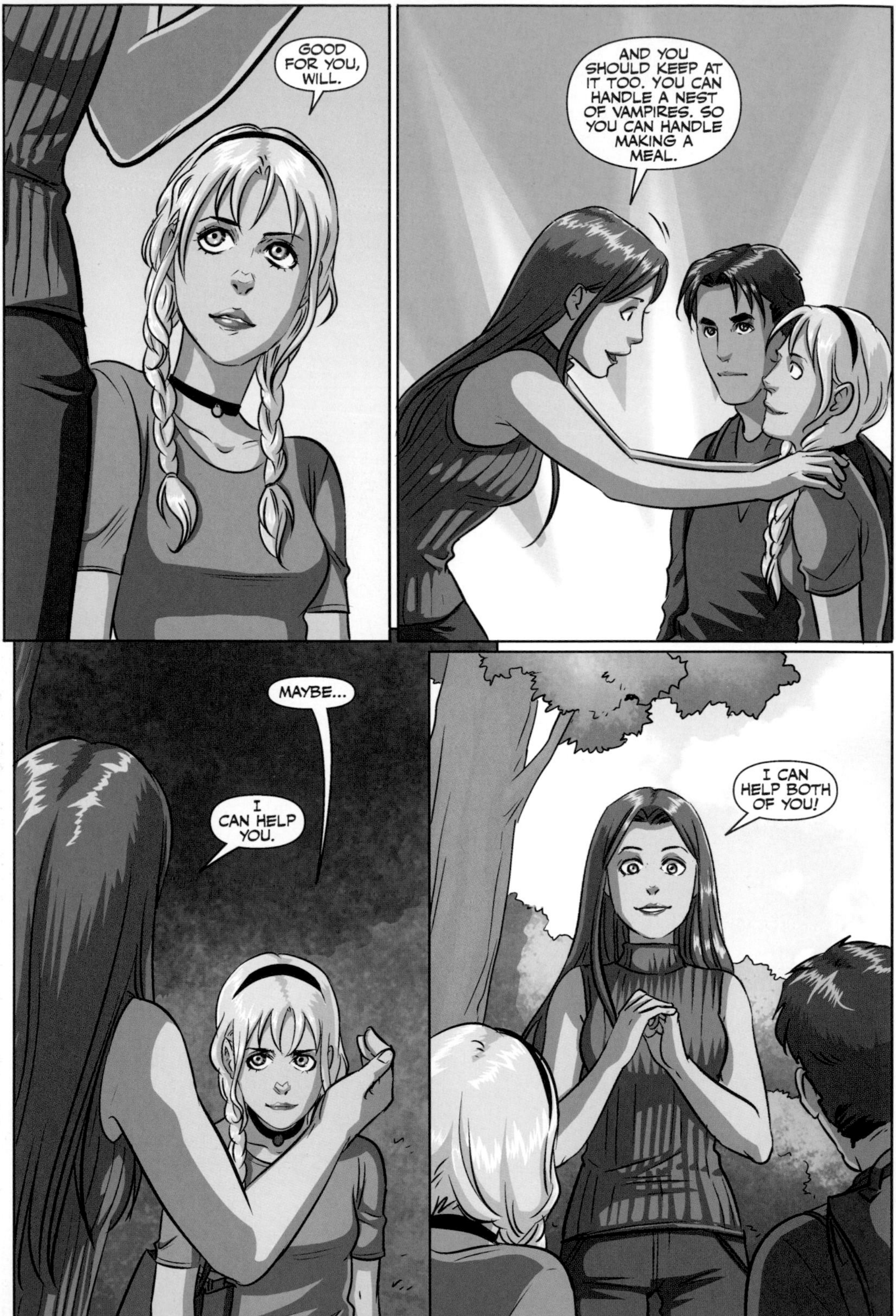
GOOD FOR YOU, WILL.
AND YOU SHOULD KEEP AT IT TOO. YOU CAN HANDLE A NEST OF VAMPIRES. SO YOU CAN HANDLE MAKING A MEAL.
MAYBE...
I CAN HELP YOU.
I CAN HELP BOTH OF YOU!

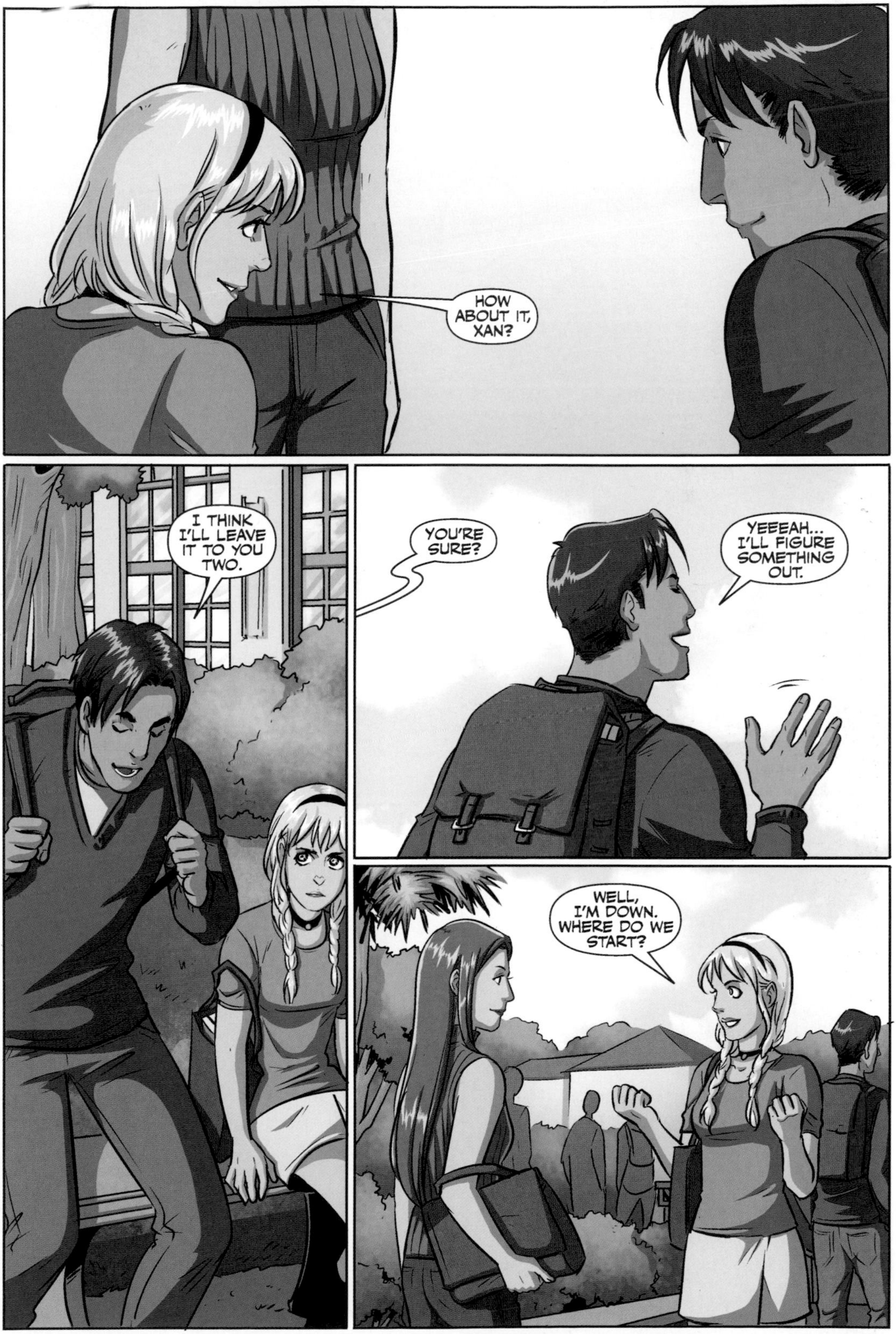

HOW ABOUT IT, XAN?
I THINK I'LL LEAVE IT TO YOU TWO.
YOU'RE SURE?
YEEEAH... I'LL FIGURE SOMETHING OUT.
WELL, I'M DOWN. WHERE DO WE START?

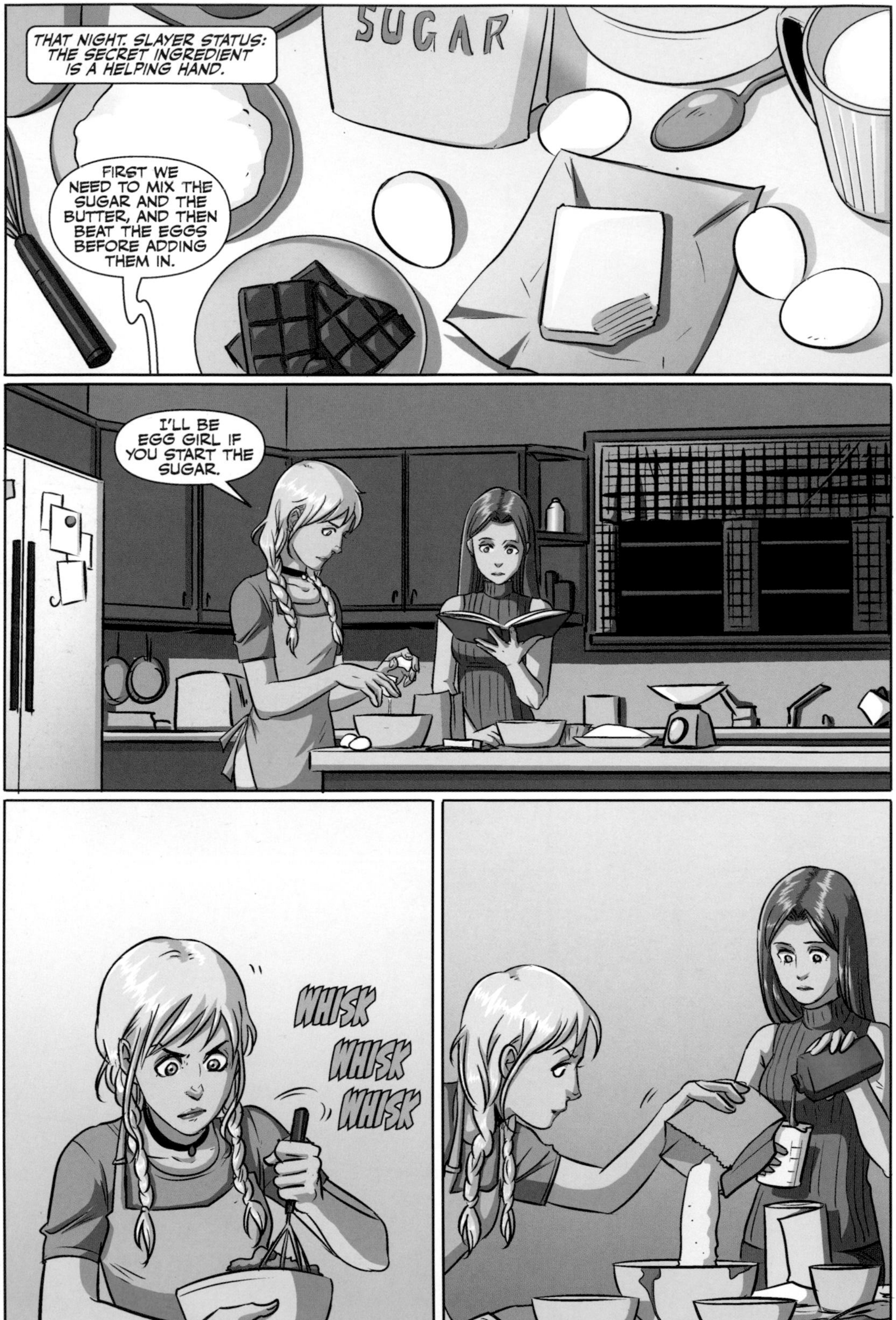
THAT NIGHT. SLAYER STATUS: THE SECRET INGREDIENT IS A HELPING HAND.
SUGAR
FIRST WE NEED TO MIX THE SUGAR AND THE BUTTER, AND THEN BEAT THE EGGS BEFORE ADDING THEM IN.
I'LL BE EGG GIRL IF YOU START THE SUGAR.
WHISK
WHISK
WHISK

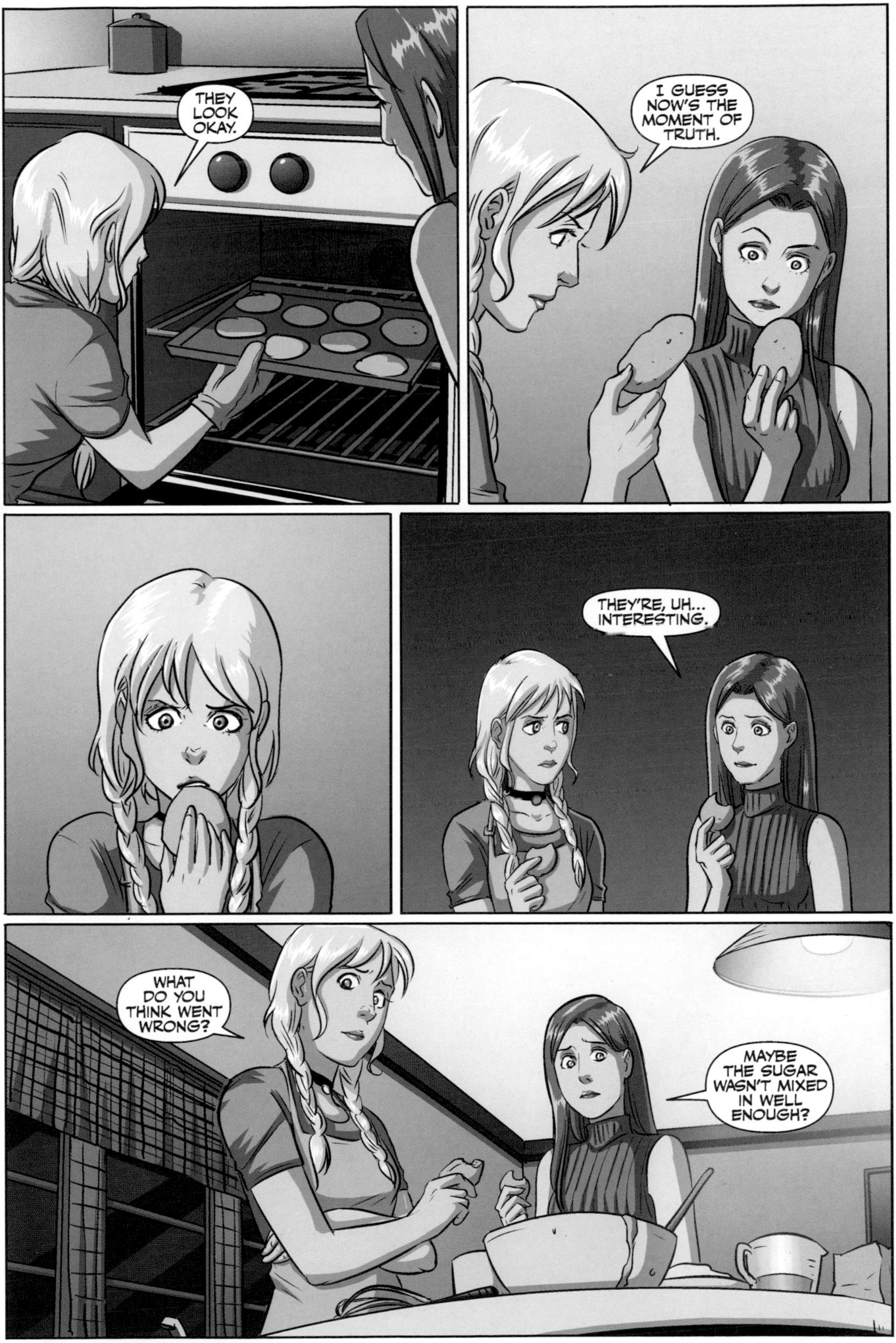
THEY LOOK OKAY.
I GUESS NOW'S THE MOMENT OF TRUTH.
THEY'RE, UH... INTERESTING.
WHAT DO YOU THINK WENT WRONG?
MAYBE THE SUGAR WASN'T MIXED IN WELL ENOUGH?

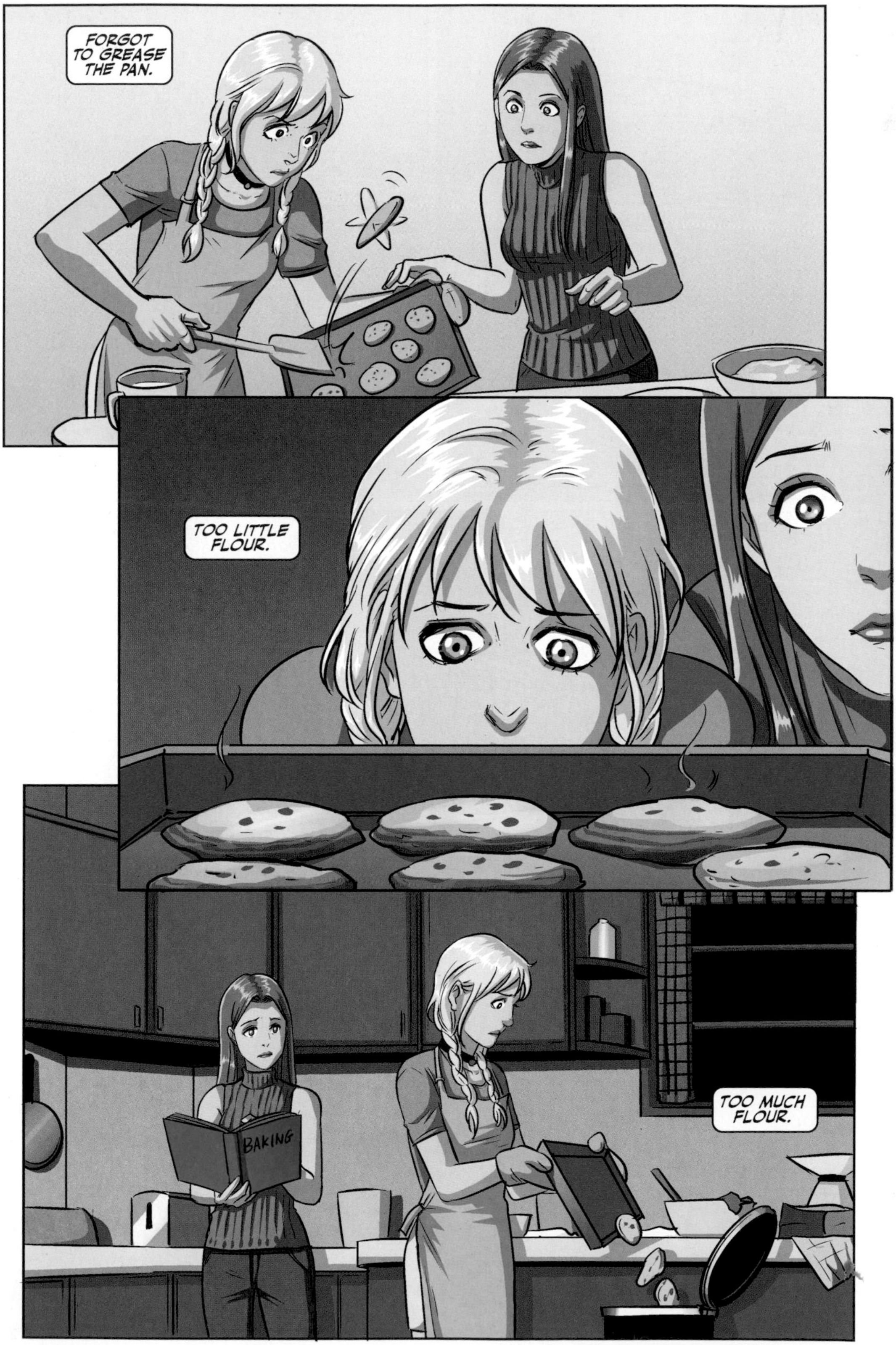
FORGOT TO GREASE THE PAN.
TOO LITTLE FLOUR.
BAKING
TOO MUCH FLOUR.

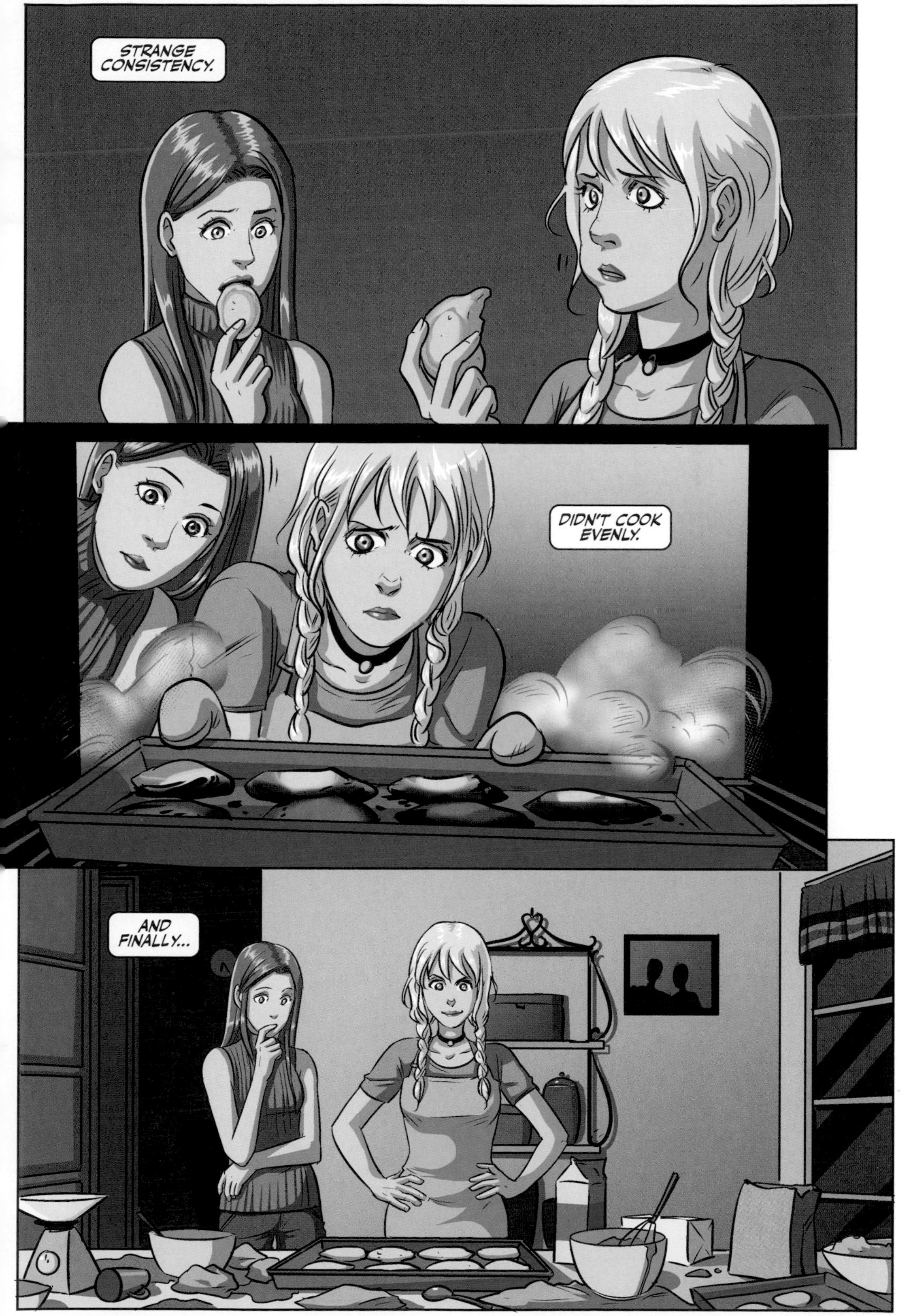
STRANGE CONSISTENCY.
DIDN'T COOK EVENLY.
AND FINALLY...

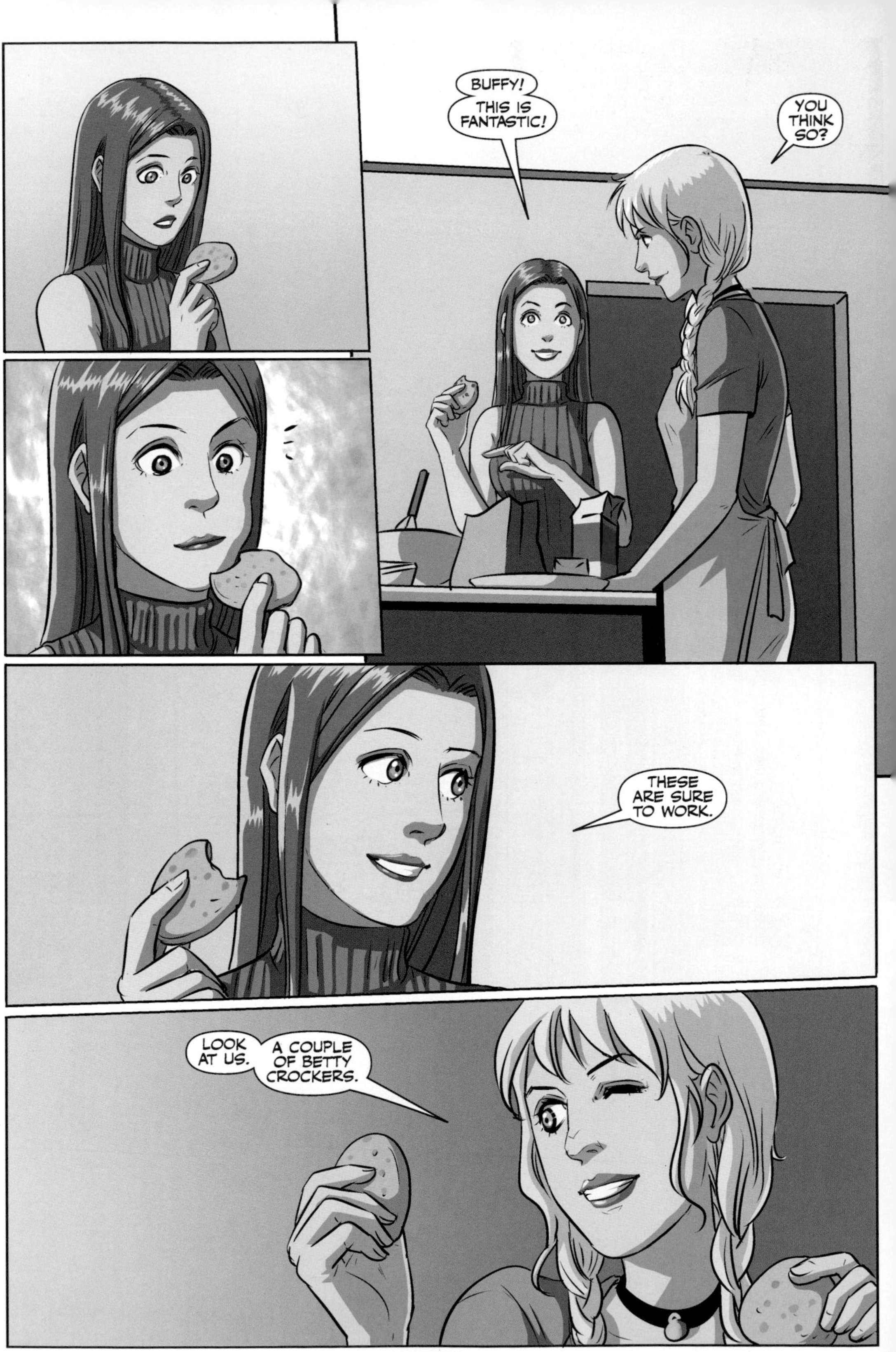
BUFFY!
THIS IS FANTASTIC!
YOU THINK SO?
THESE ARE SURE TO WORK.
LOOK AT US.
A COUPLE OF BETTY CROCKERS.

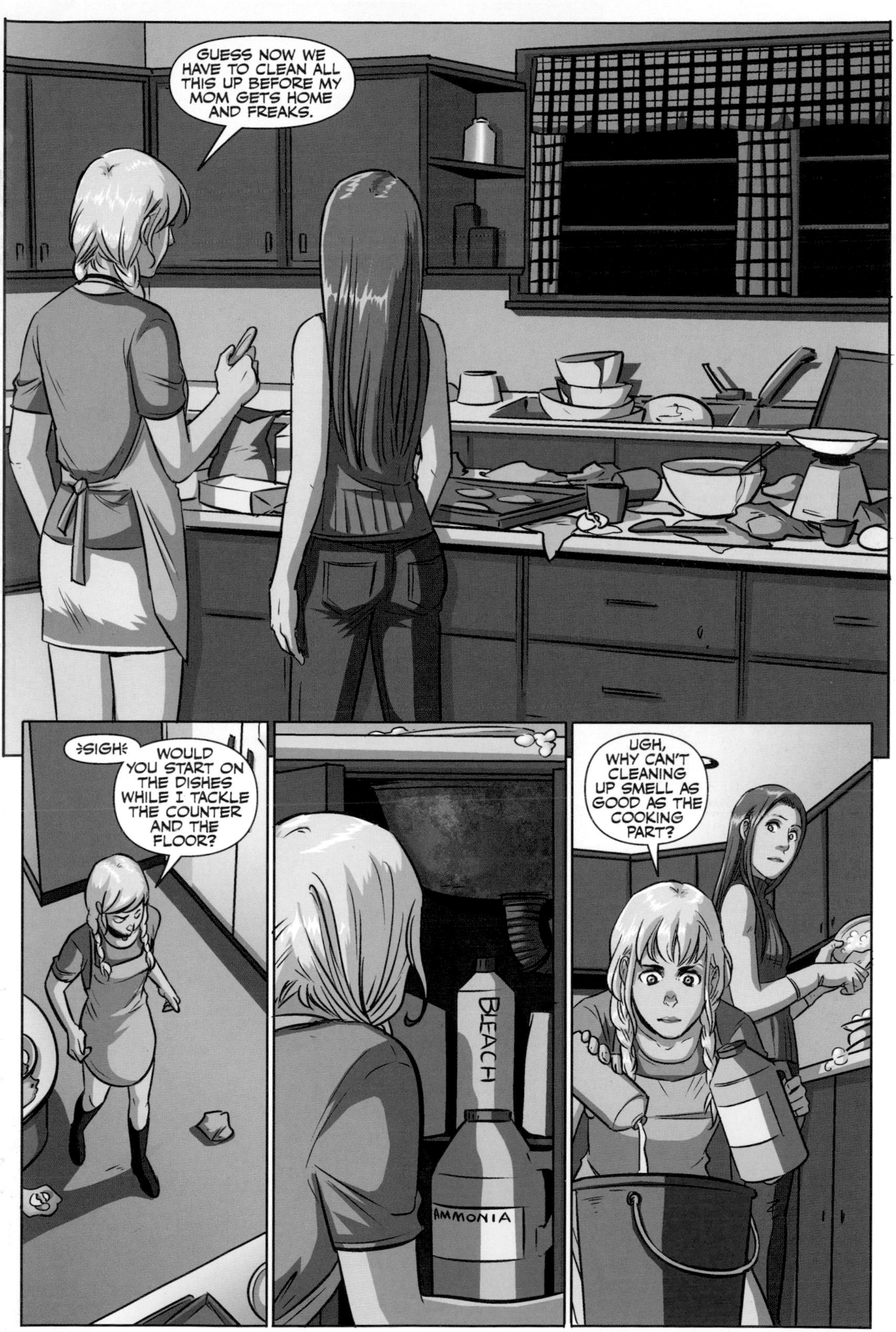
GUESS NOW WE HAVE TO CLEAN ALL THIS UP BEFORE MY MOM GETS HOME AND FREAKS.
SIGH
WOULD YOU START ON THE DISHES WHILE I TACKLE THE COUNTER AND THE FLOOR?
BLEACH
AMMONIA
UGH, WHY CAN'T CLEANING UP SMELL AS GOOD AS THE COOKING PART?

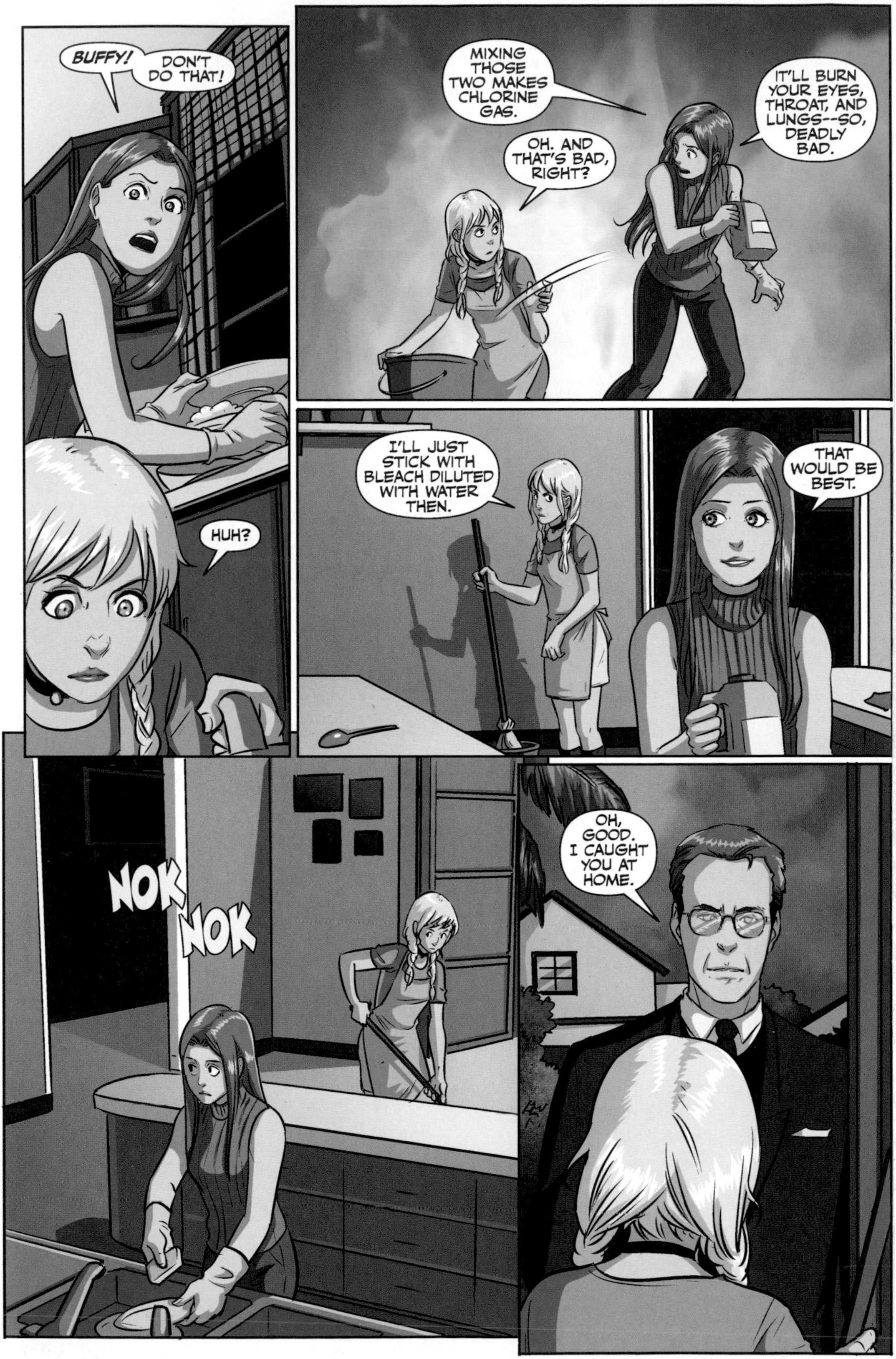

BUFFY!
DON'T DO THAT!
HUH?
MIXING THOSE TWO MAKES CHLORINE GAS.
OH. AND THAT'S BAD, RIGHT?
IT'LL BURN YOUR EYES, THROAT, AND LUNGS--SO, DEADLY BAD.
I'LL JUST STICK WITH BLEACH DILUTED WITH WATER THEN.
THAT WOULD BE BEST.
NOK NOK
OH, GOOD. I CAUGHT YOU AT HOME.

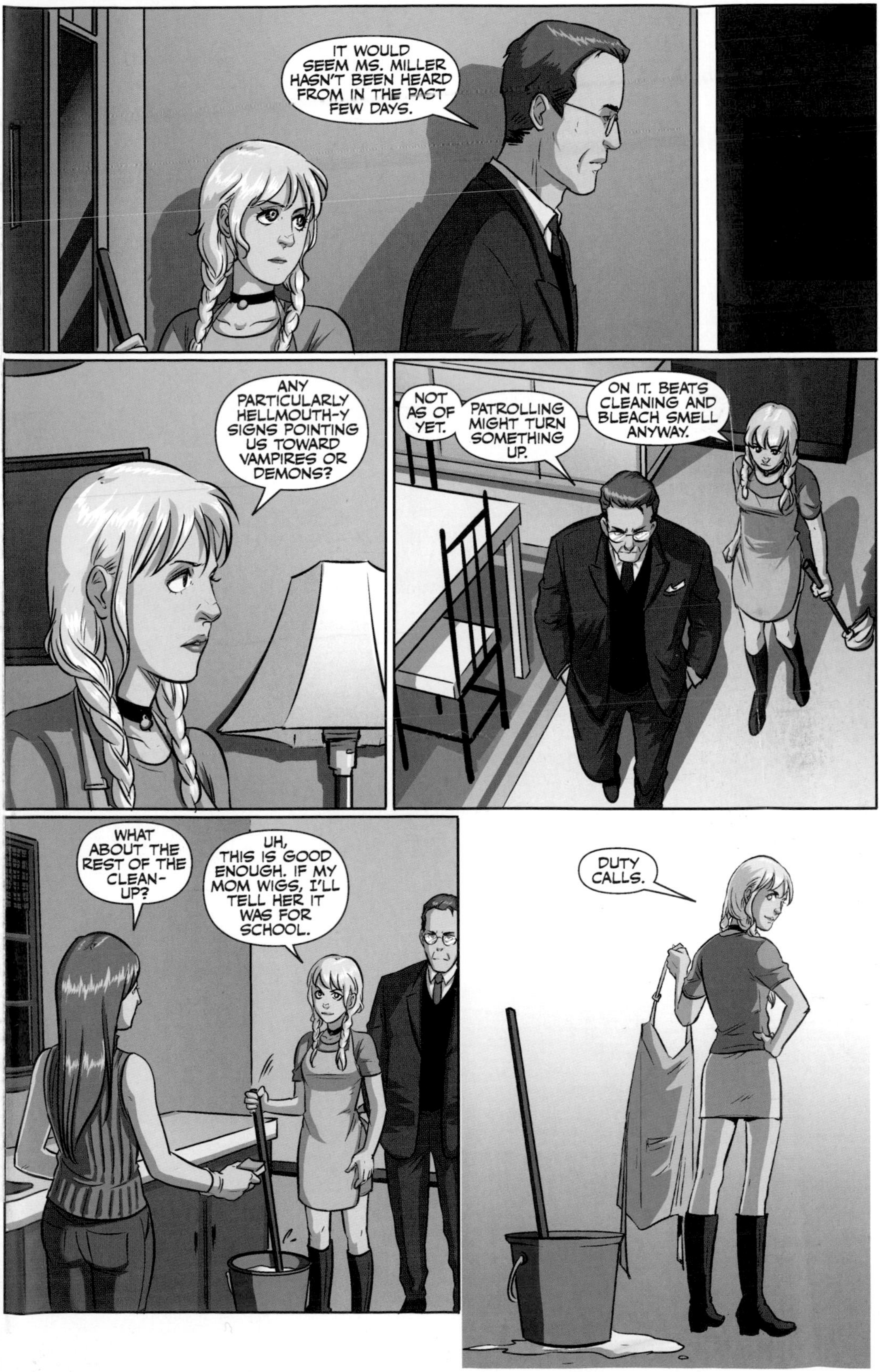
IT WOULD SEEM MS. MILLER HASN'T BEEN HEARD FROM IN THE PAST FEW DAYS.
ANY PARTICULARLY HELLMOUTH-Y SIGNS POINTING US TOWARD VAMPIRES OR DEMONS?
NOT AS OF YET.
PATROLLING MIGHT TURN SOMETHING UP.
ON IT. BEATS CLEANING AND BLEACH SMELL ANYWAY.
WHAT ABOUT THE REST OF THE CLEAN-UP?
UH, THIS IS GOOD ENOUGH. IF MY MOM WIGS, I'LL TELL HER IT WAS FOR SCHOOL.
DUTY CALLS.

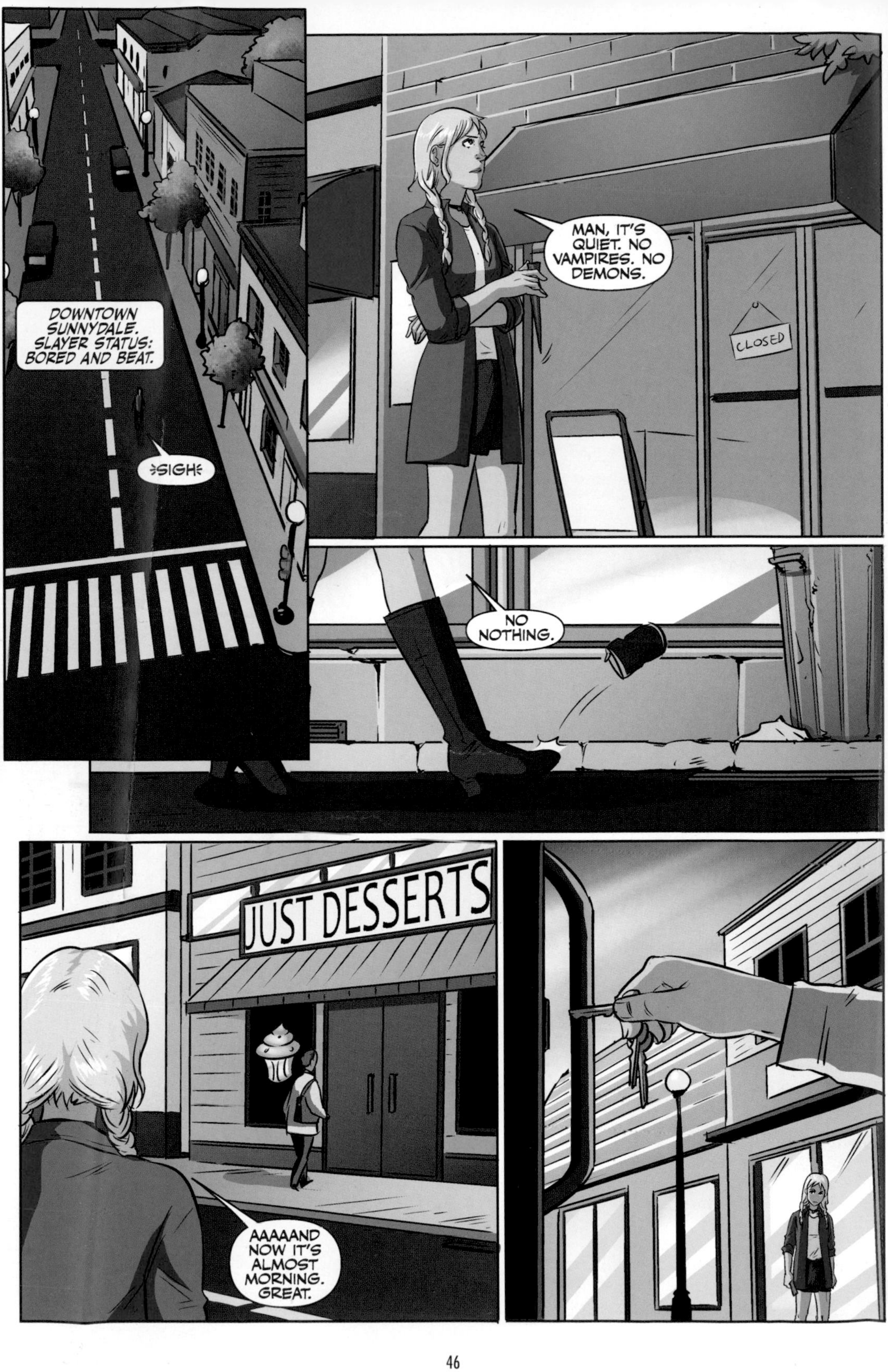
DOWNTOWN SUNNYDALE. SLAYER STATUS: BORED AND BEAT.
SIGH
MAN, IT'S QUIET. NO VAMPIRES. NO DEMONS.
CLOSED
NO NOTHING.
JUST DESSERTS
AAAAAND NOW IT'S ALMOST MORNING. GREAT.

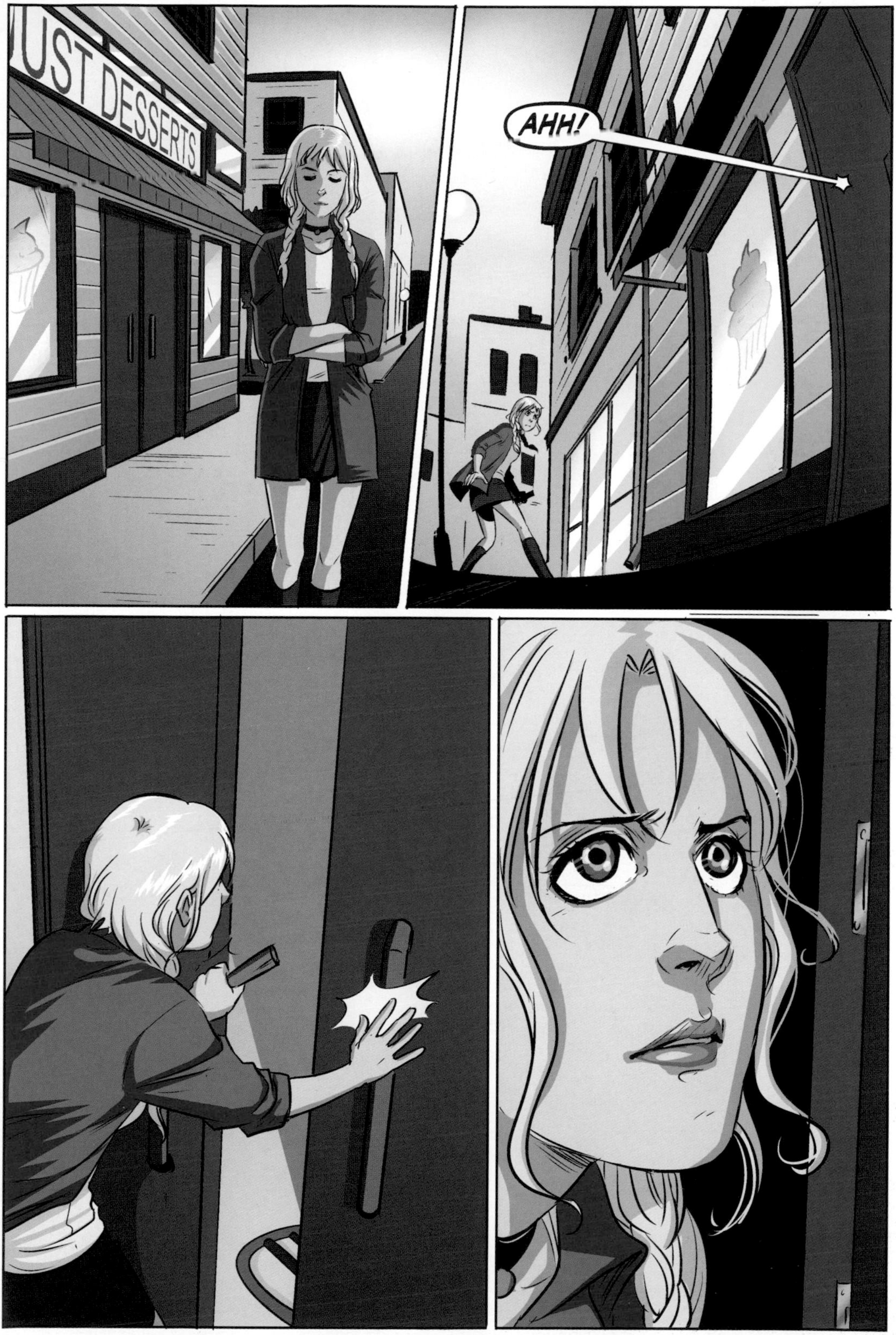
UST DESSERTS
AHH!

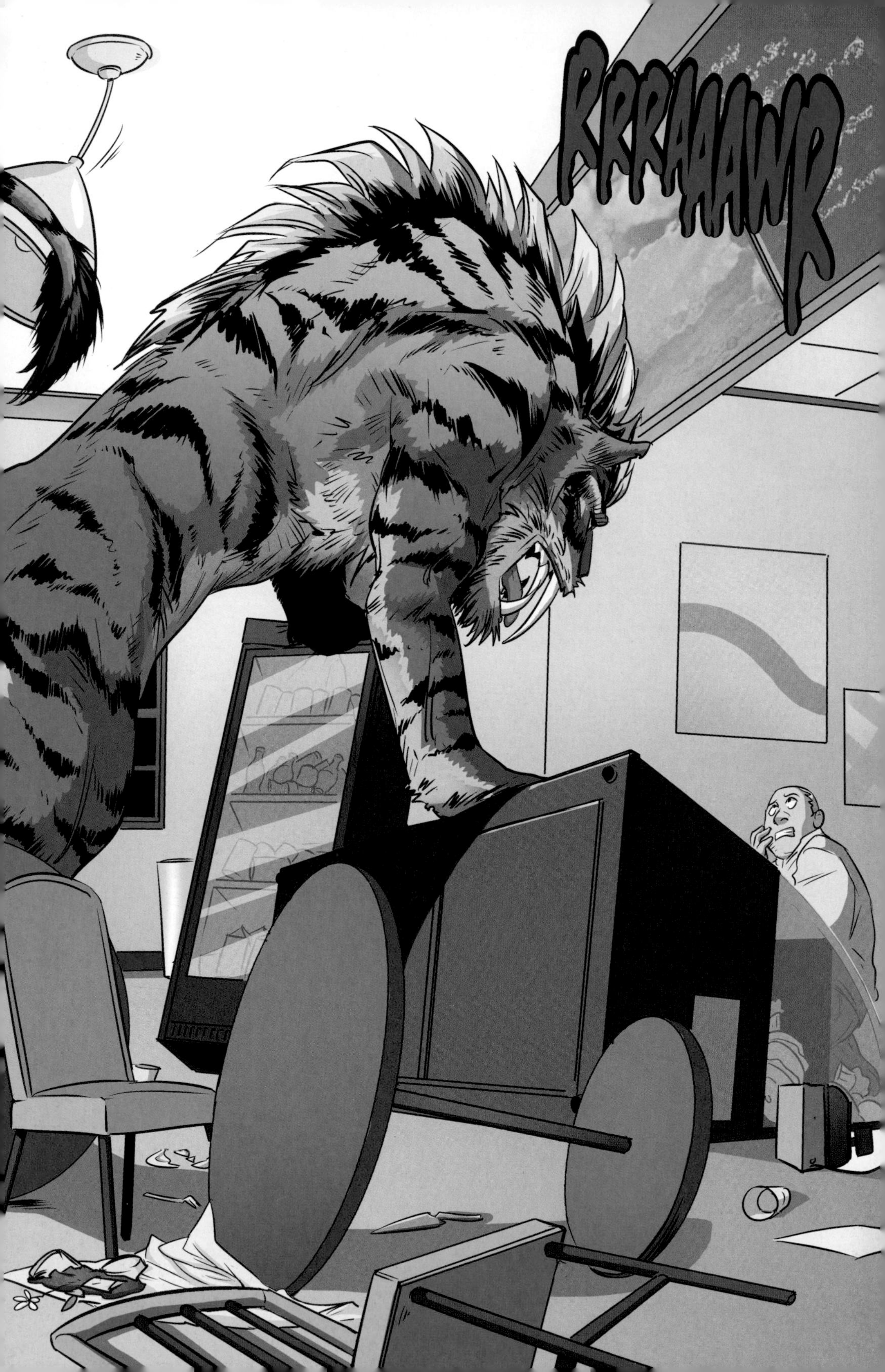
RRRAAAWR

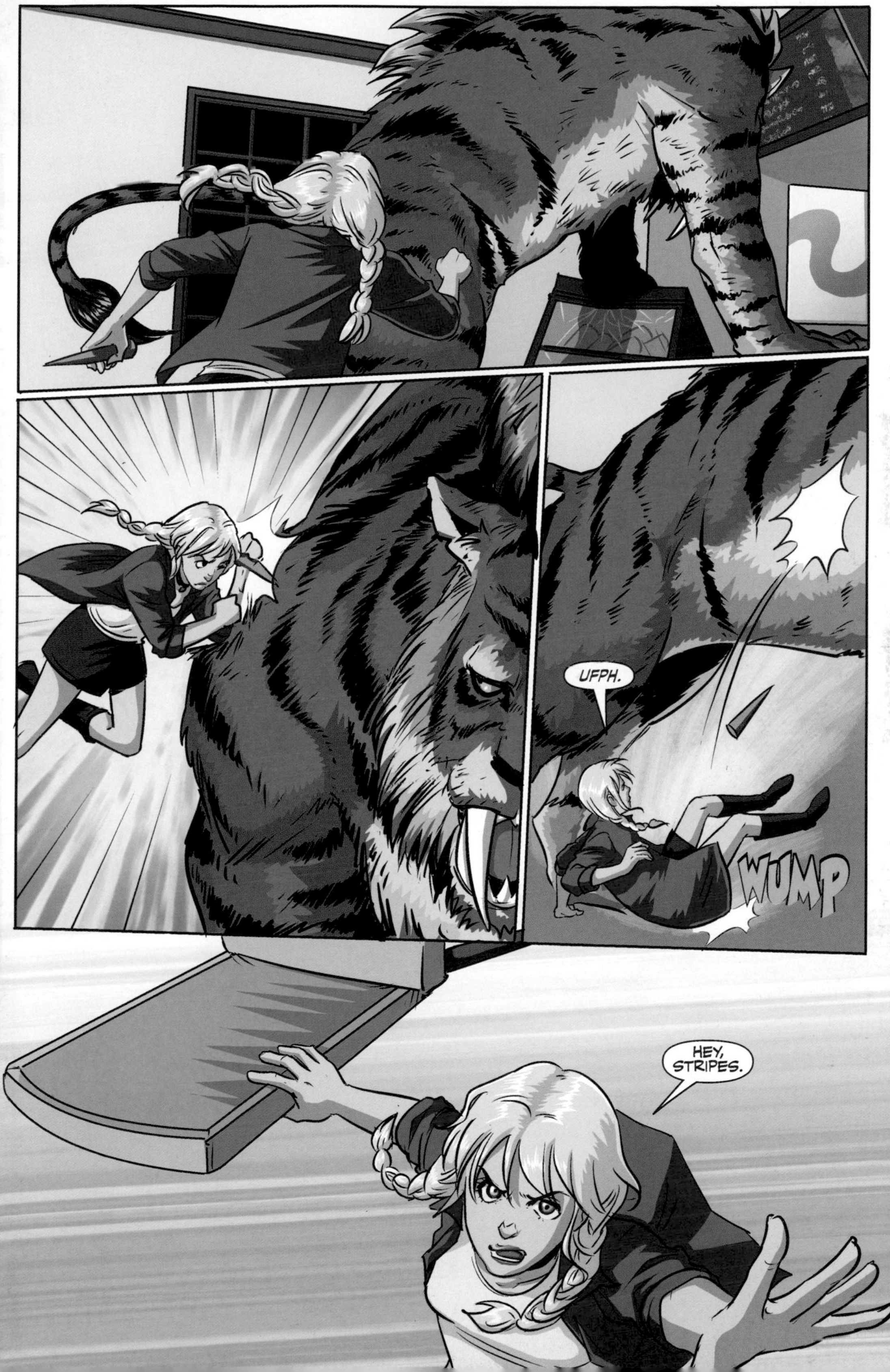
UFPH.
WUMP
HEY, STRIPES.

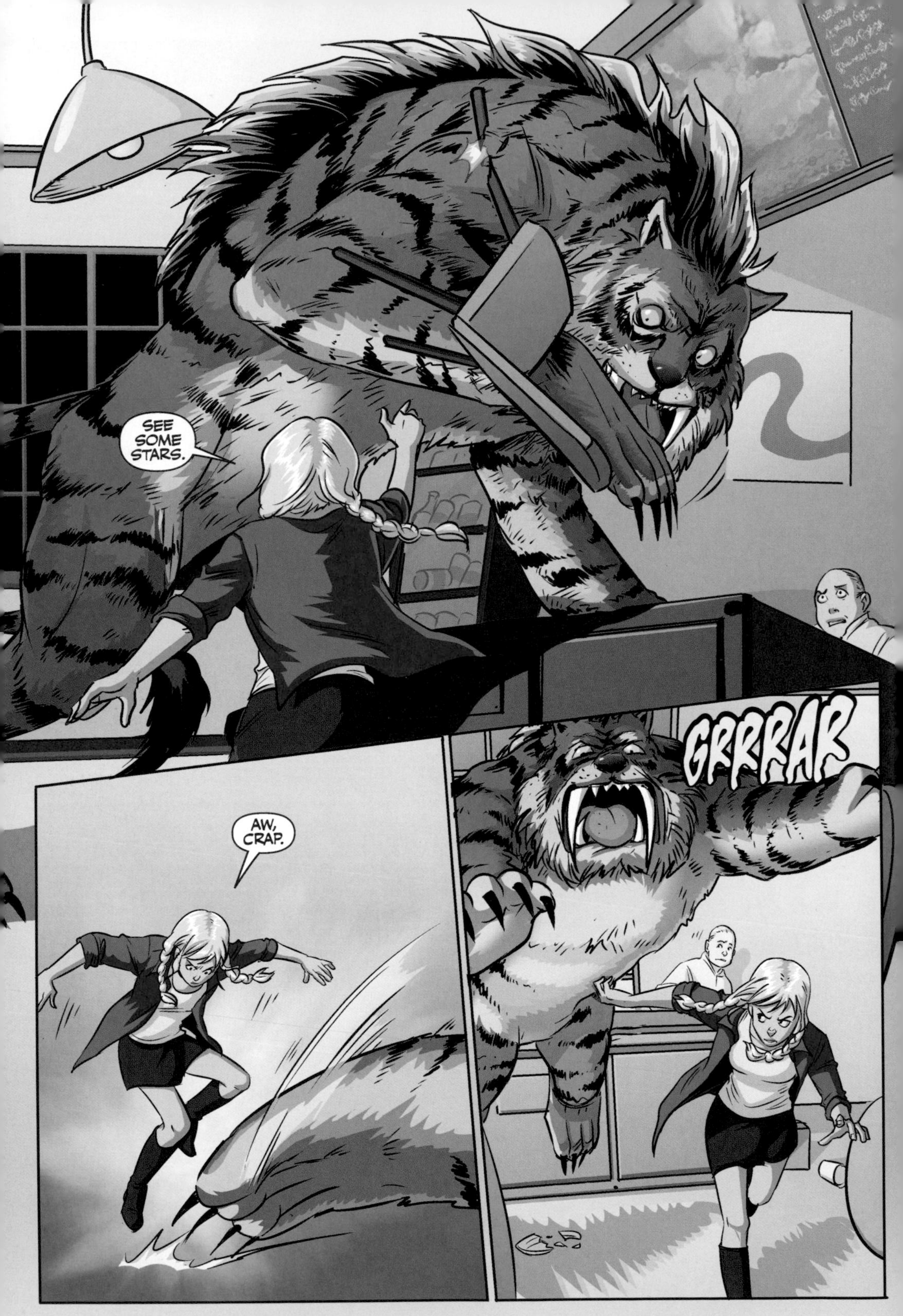
SEE SOME STARS.
GRRRAR
AW, CRAP.

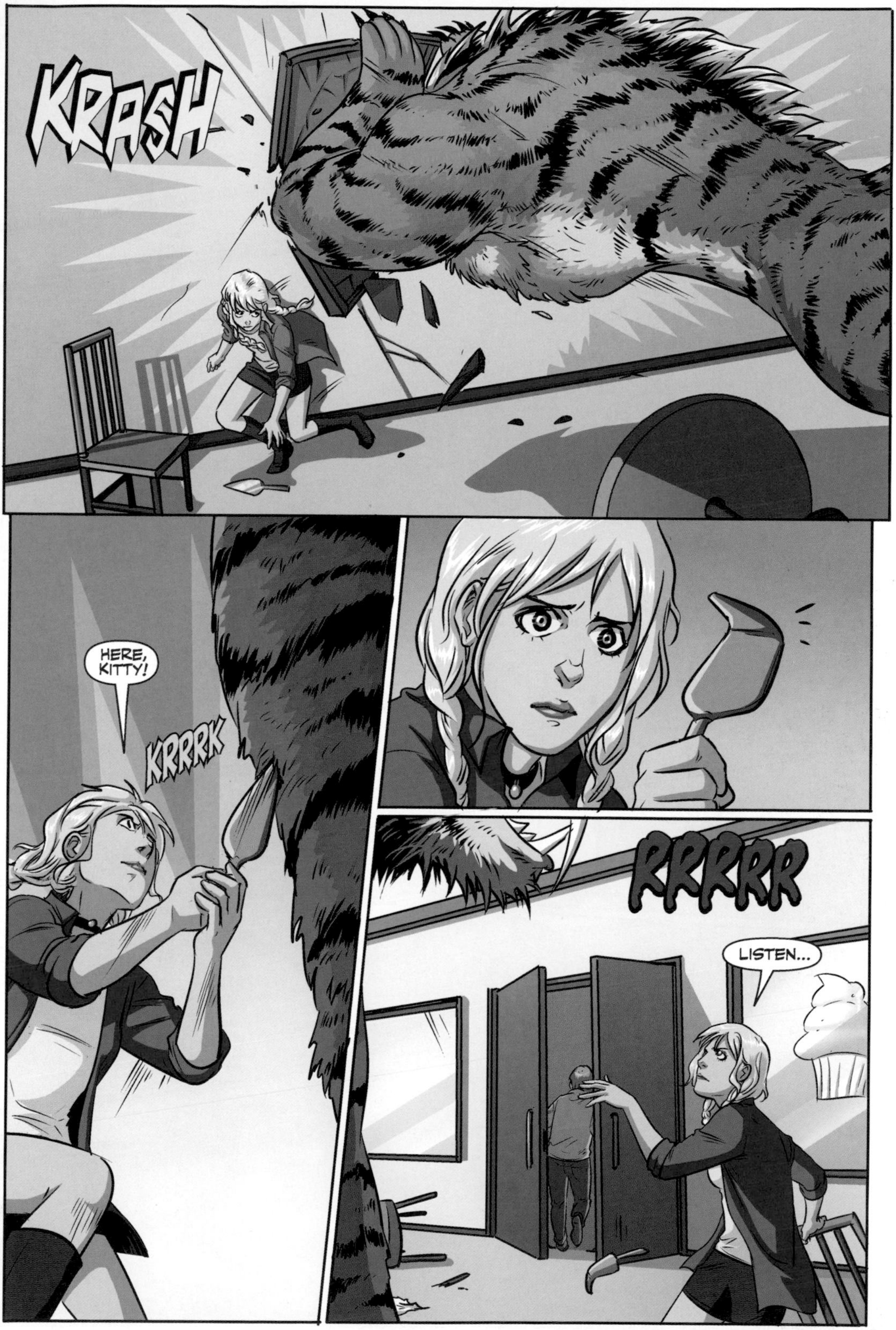
KRASH
HERE, KITTY!
KRRRK
RRRRR
LISTEN...

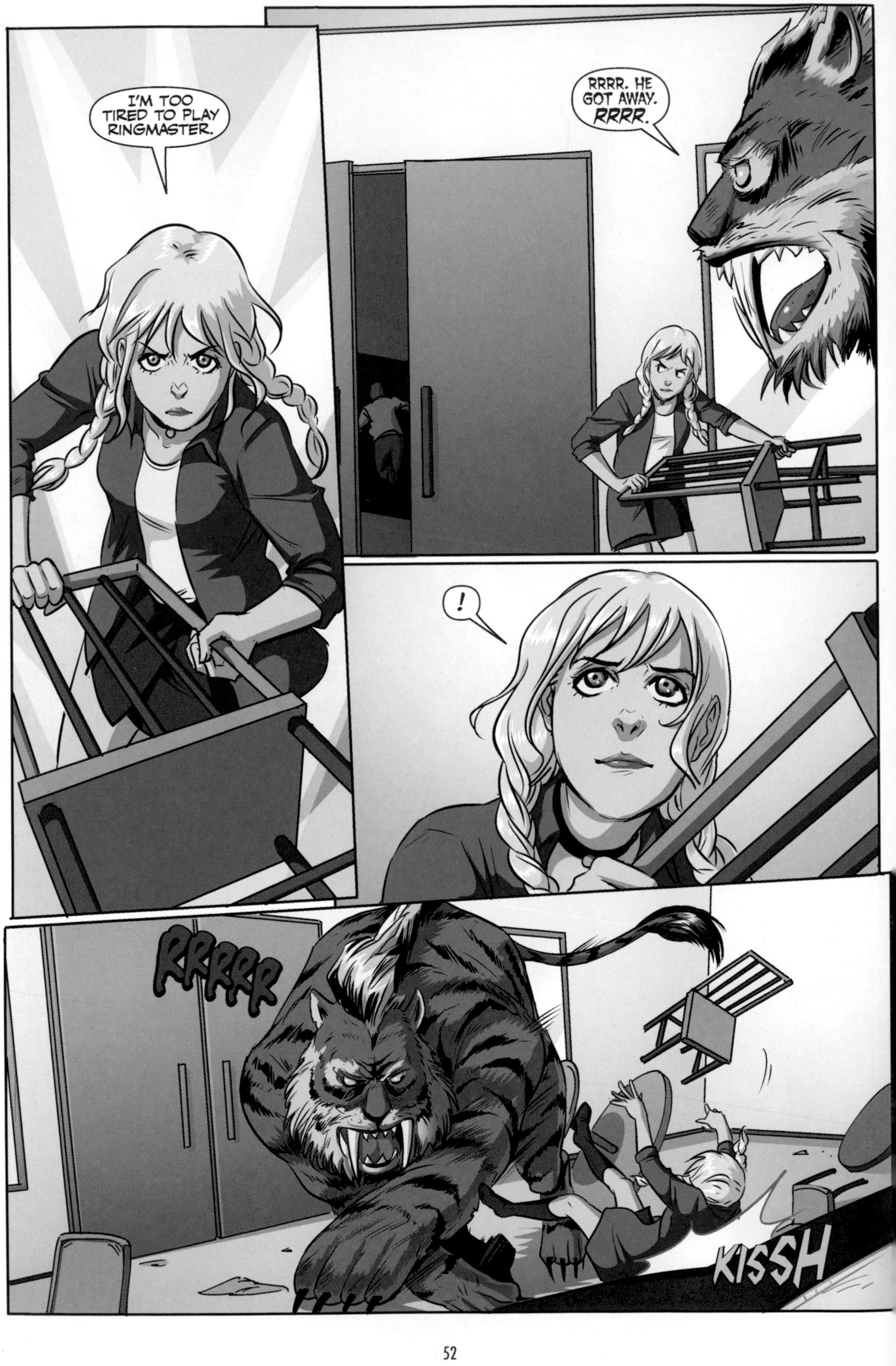
I'M TOO TIRED TO PLAY RINGMASTER.
RRRR. HE GOT AWAY. RRRR.
!
RRRRR
KISSH

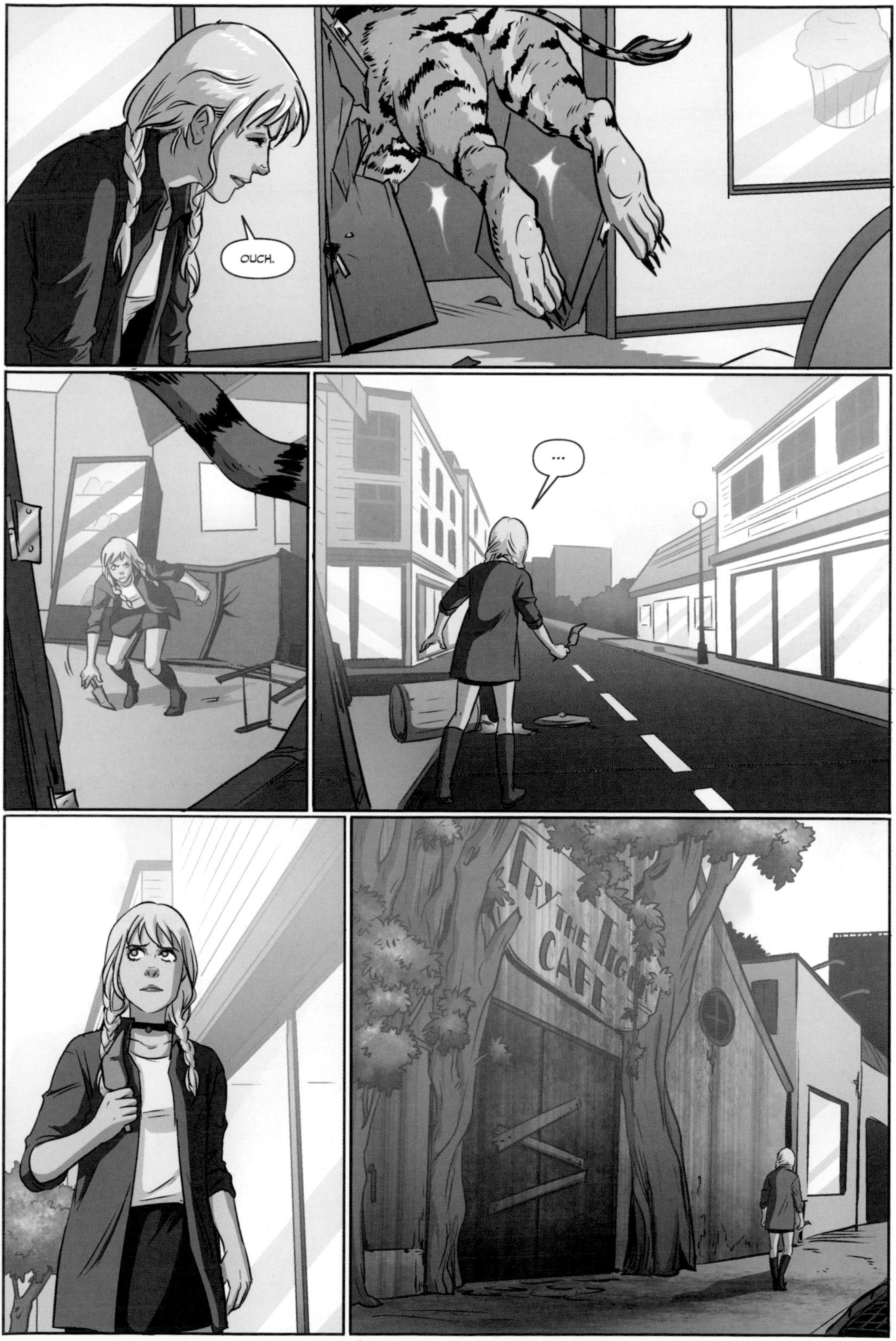
OUCH.
...
FRY THE TIG
CAFE

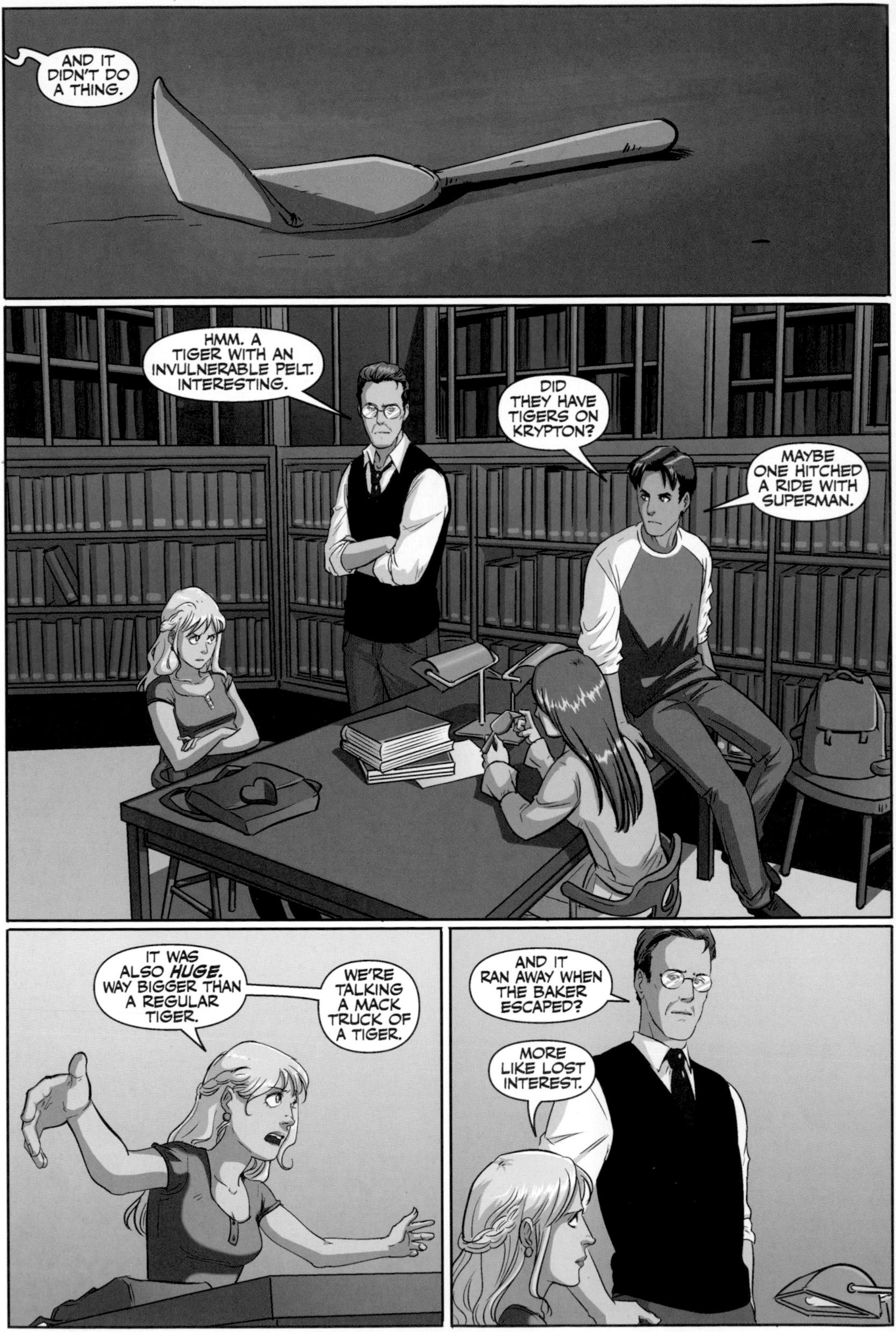
AND IT DIDN'T DO A THING.
HMM. A TIGER WITH AN INVULNERABLE PELT. INTERESTING.
DID THEY HAVE TIGERS ON KRYPTON?
MAYBE ONE HITCHED A RIDE WITH SUPERMAN.
IT WAS ALSO HUGE. WAY BIGGER THAN A REGULAR TIGER.
WE'RE TALKING A MACK TRUCK OF A TIGER.
AND IT RAN AWAY WHEN THE BAKER ESCAPED?
MORE LIKE LOST INTEREST.

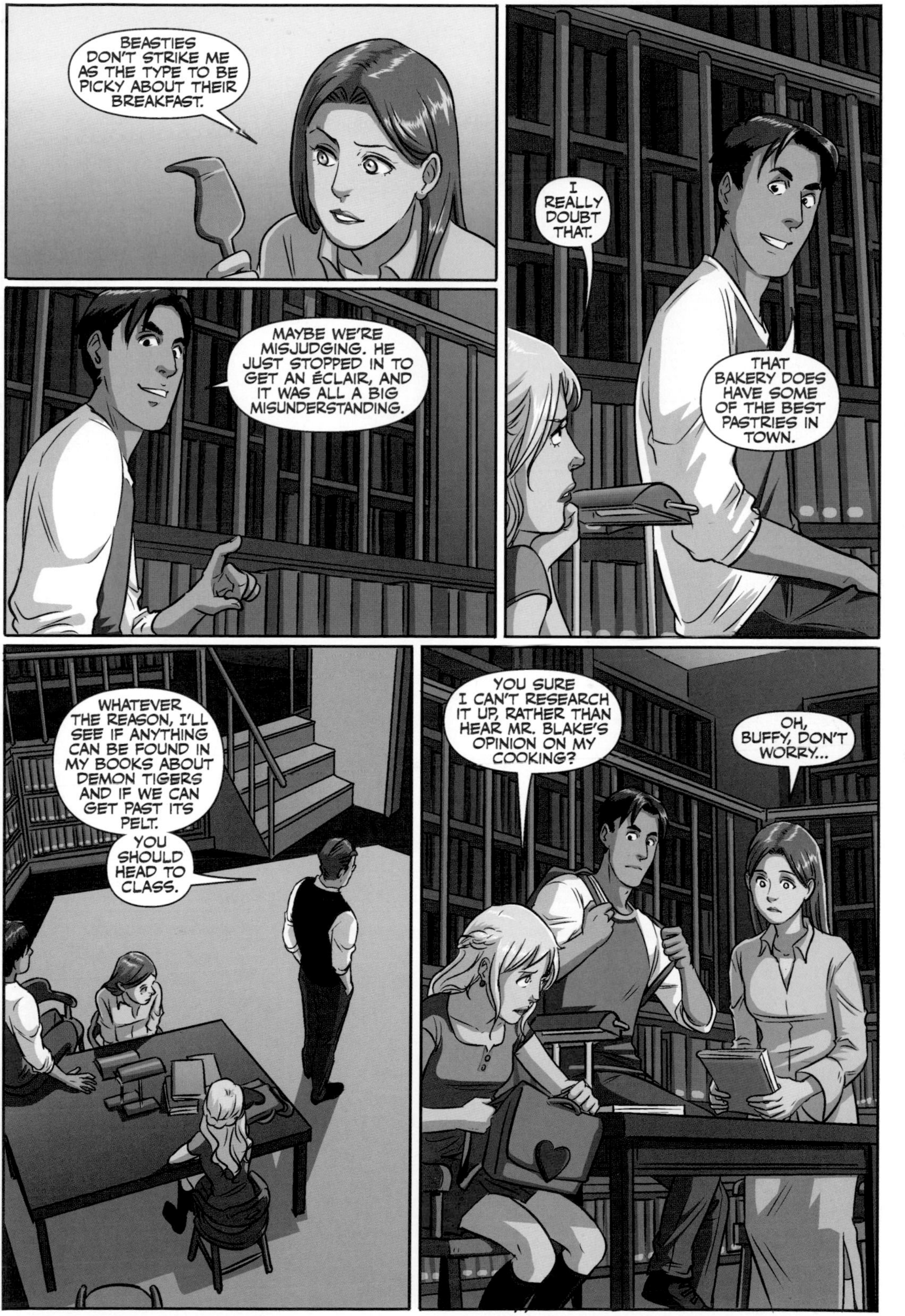
BEASTIES DON'T STRIKE ME AS THE TYPE TO BE PICKY ABOUT THEIR BREAKFAST.
I REALLY DOUBT THAT.
MAYBE WE'RE MISJUDGING. HE JUST STOPPED IN TO GET AN ÉCLAIR, AND IT WAS ALL A BIG MISUNDERSTANDING.
THAT BAKERY DOES HAVE SOME OF THE BEST PASTRIES IN TOWN.
WHATEVER THE REASON, I'LL SEE IF ANYTHING CAN BE FOUND IN MY BOOKS ABOUT DEMON TIGERS AND IF WE CAN GET PAST ITS PELT.
YOU SHOULD HEAD TO CLASS.
YOU SURE I CAN'T RESEARCH IT UP, RATHER THAN HEAR MR. BLAKE'S OPINION ON MY COOKING?
OH, BUFFY, DON'T WORRY...

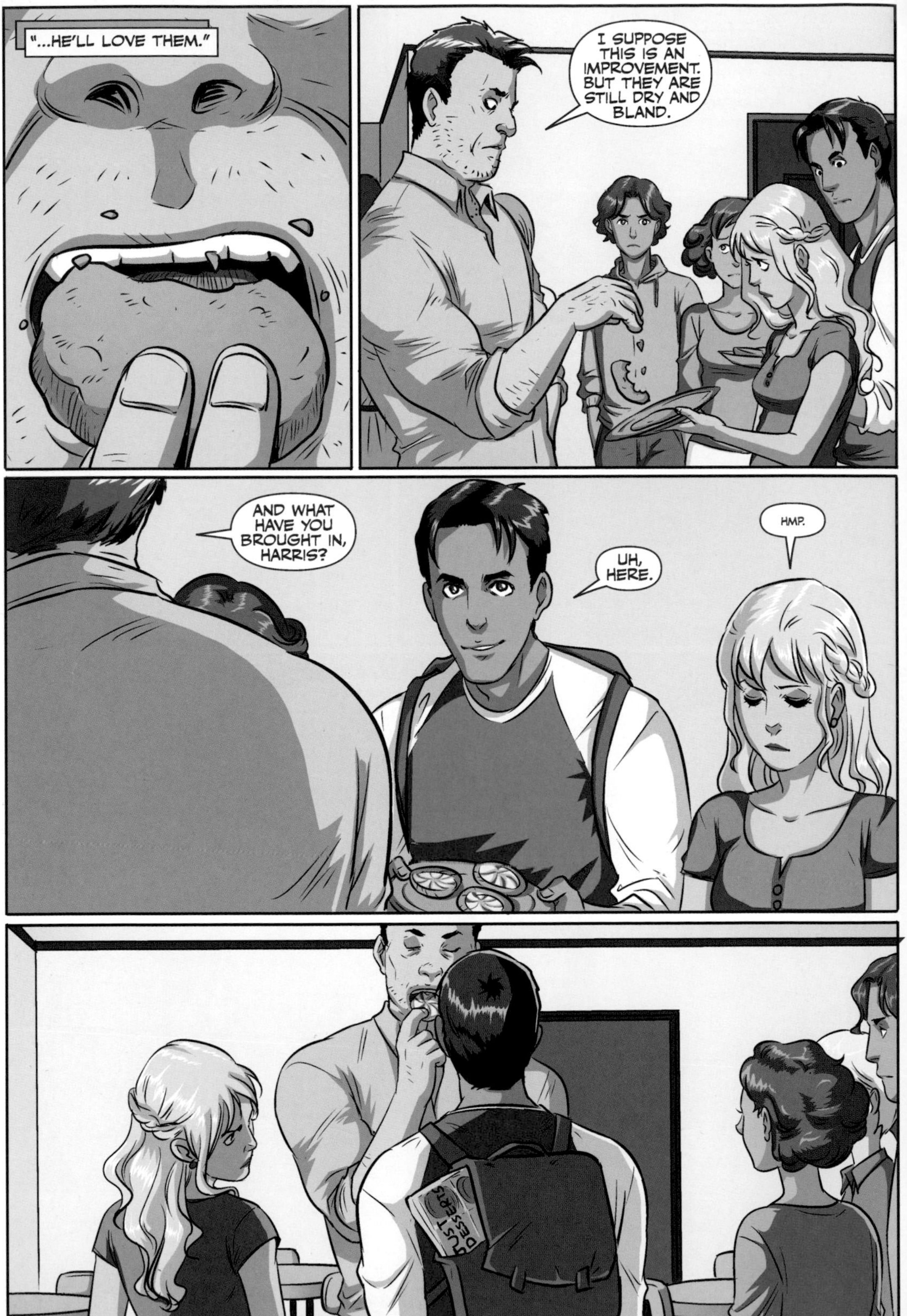
"...HE'LL LOVE THEM."
I SUPPOSE THIS IS AN IMPROVEMENT. BUT THEY ARE STILL DRY AND BLAND.
AND WHAT HAVE YOU BROUGHT IN, HARRIS?
UH, HERE.
HMP.
JUST DESSERTS

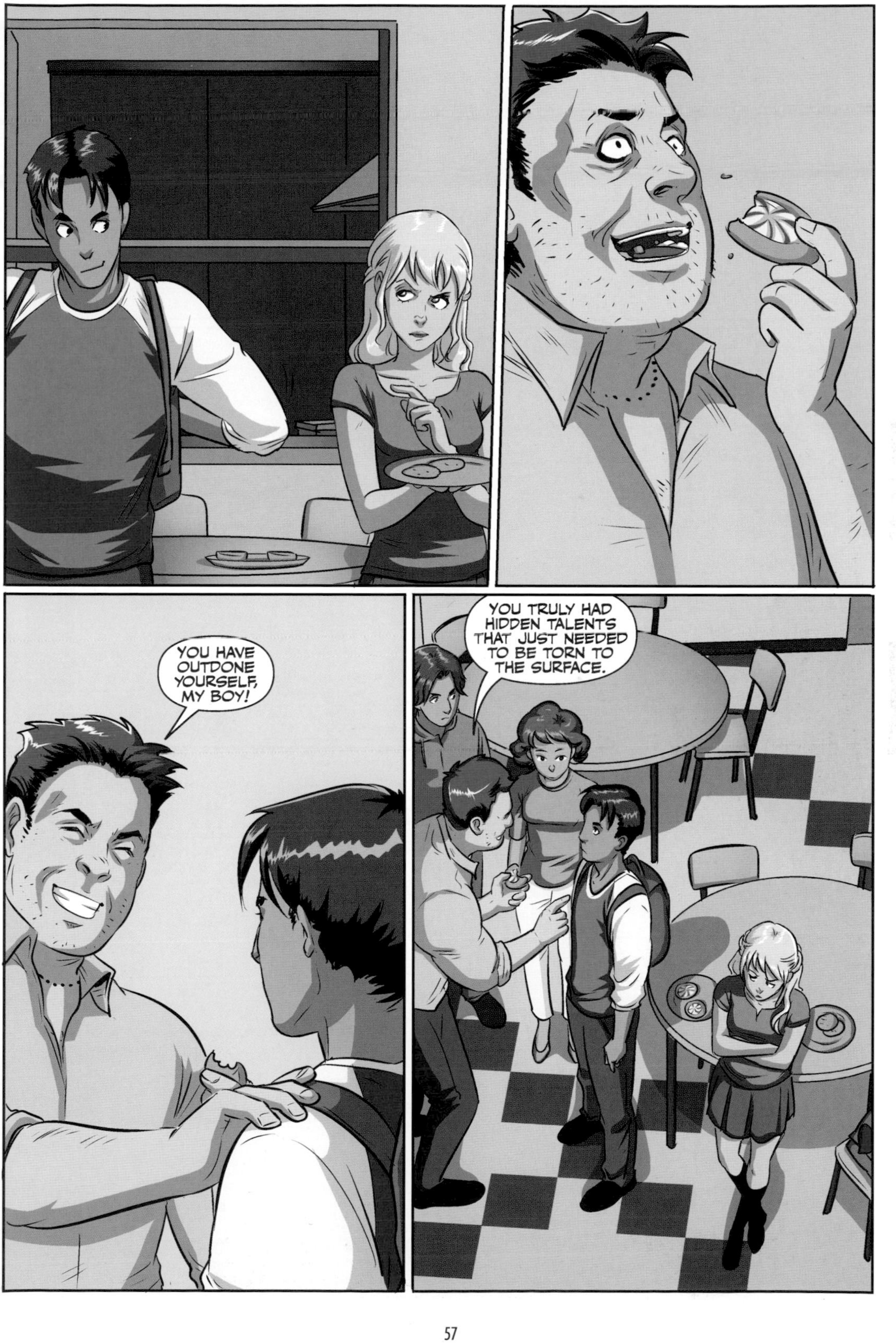
YOU HAVE OUTDONE YOURSELF, MY BOY!
YOU TRULY HAD HIDDEN TALENTS THAT JUST NEEDED TO BE TORN TO THE SURFACE.

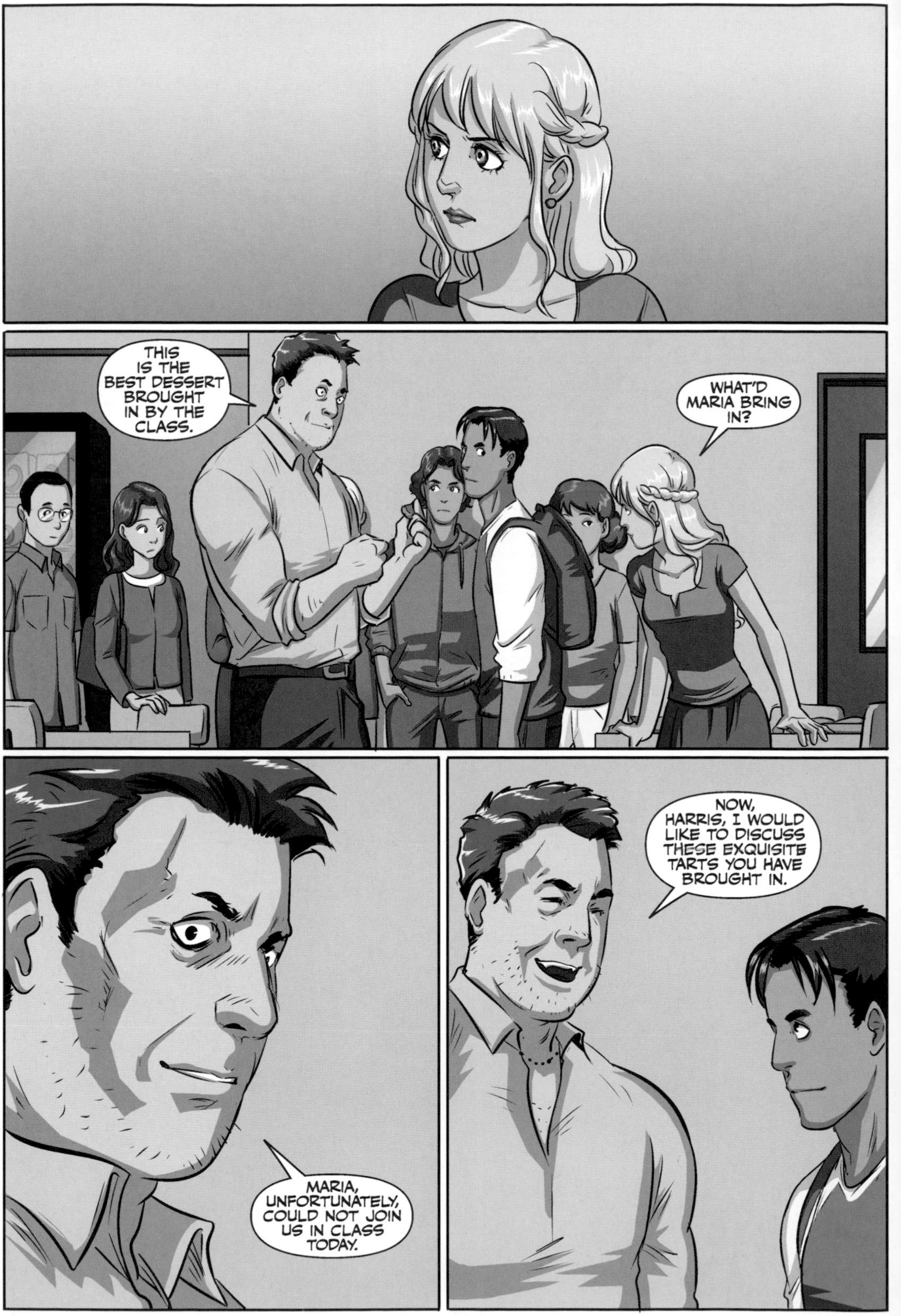
THIS IS THE BEST DESSERT BROUGHT IN BY THE CLASS.
WHAT'D MARIA BRING IN?
MARIA, UNFORTUNATELY, COULD NOT JOIN US IN CLASS TODAY.
NOW, HARRIS, I WOULD LIKE TO DISCUSS THESE EXQUISITE TARTS YOU HAVE BROUGHT IN.

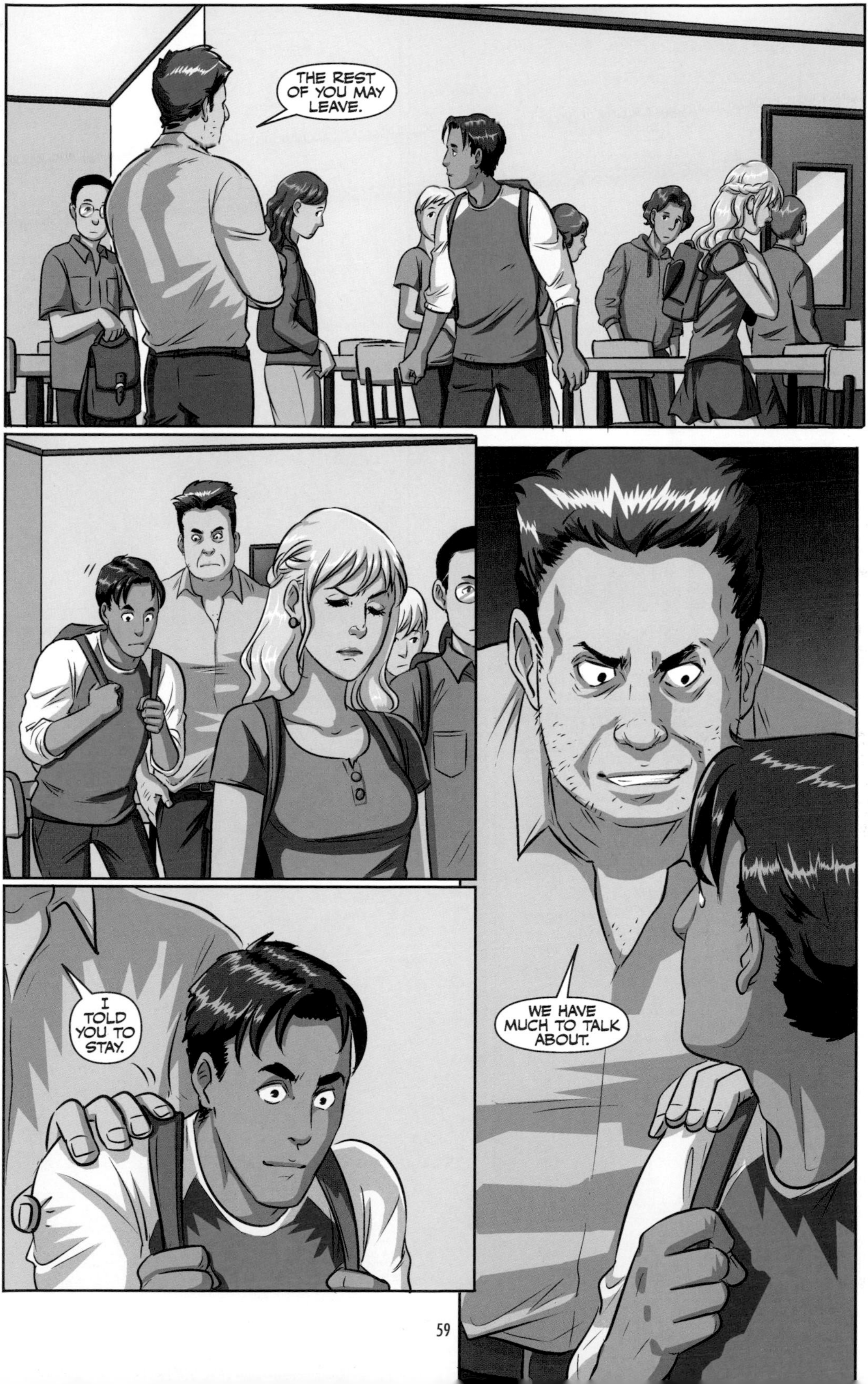
THE REST OF YOU MAY LEAVE.
I TOLD YOU TO STAY.
WE HAVE MUCH TO TALK ABOUT.

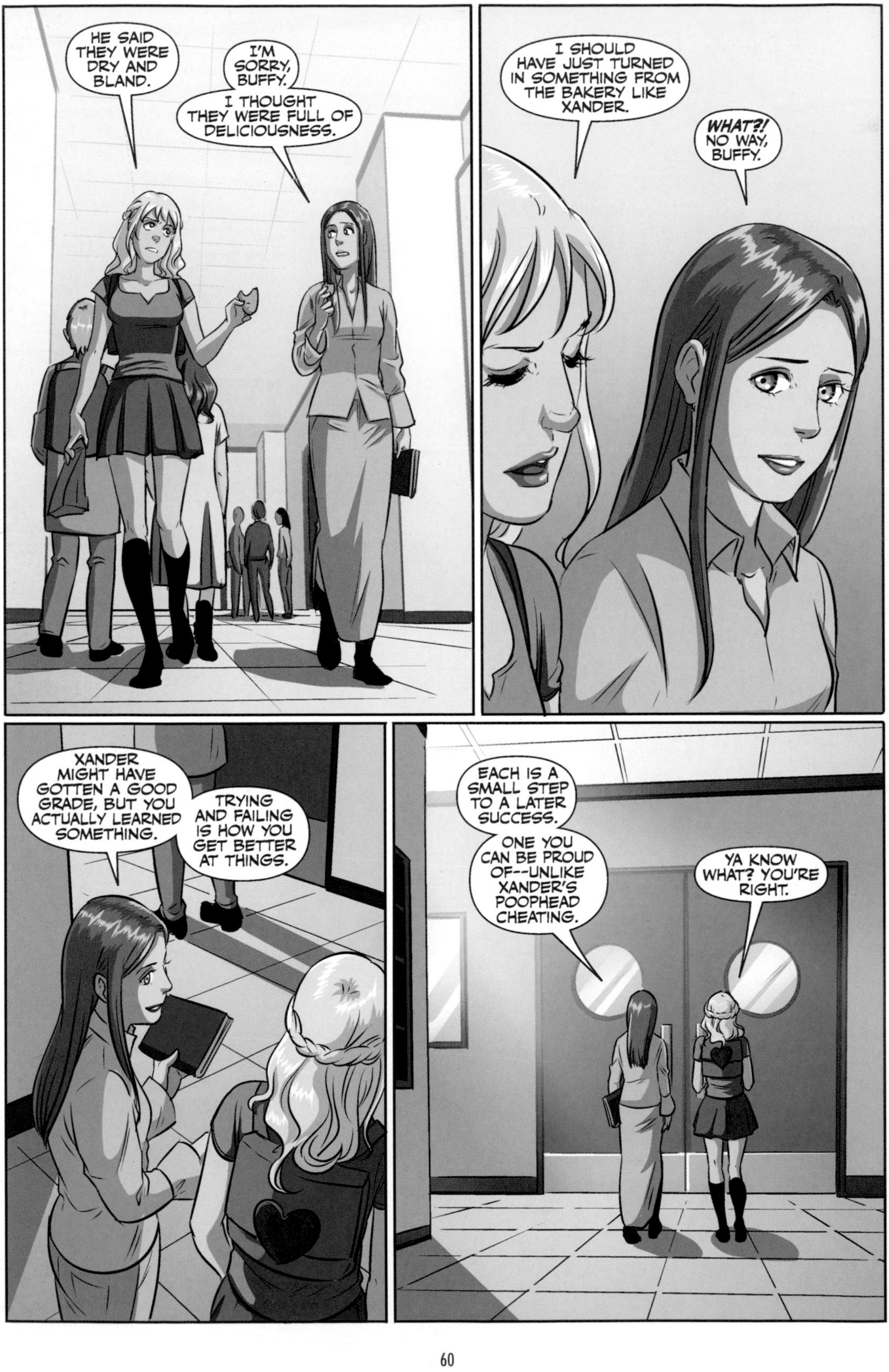
HE SAID THEY WERE DRY AND BLAND.
I'M SORRY, BUFFY.
I THOUGHT THEY WERE FULL OF DELICIOUSNESS.
I SHOULD HAVE JUST TURNED IN SOMETHING FROM THE BAKERY LIKE XANDER.
WHAT?! NO WAY, BUFFY.
XANDER MIGHT HAVE GOTTEN A GOOD GRADE, BUT YOU ACTUALLY LEARNED SOMETHING.
TRYING AND FAILING IS HOW YOU GET BETTER AT THINGS.
EACH IS A SMALL STEP TO A LATER SUCCESS.
ONE YOU CAN BE PROUD OF--UNLIKE XANDER'S POOPHEAD CHEATING.
YA KNOW WHAT? YOU'RE RIGHT.

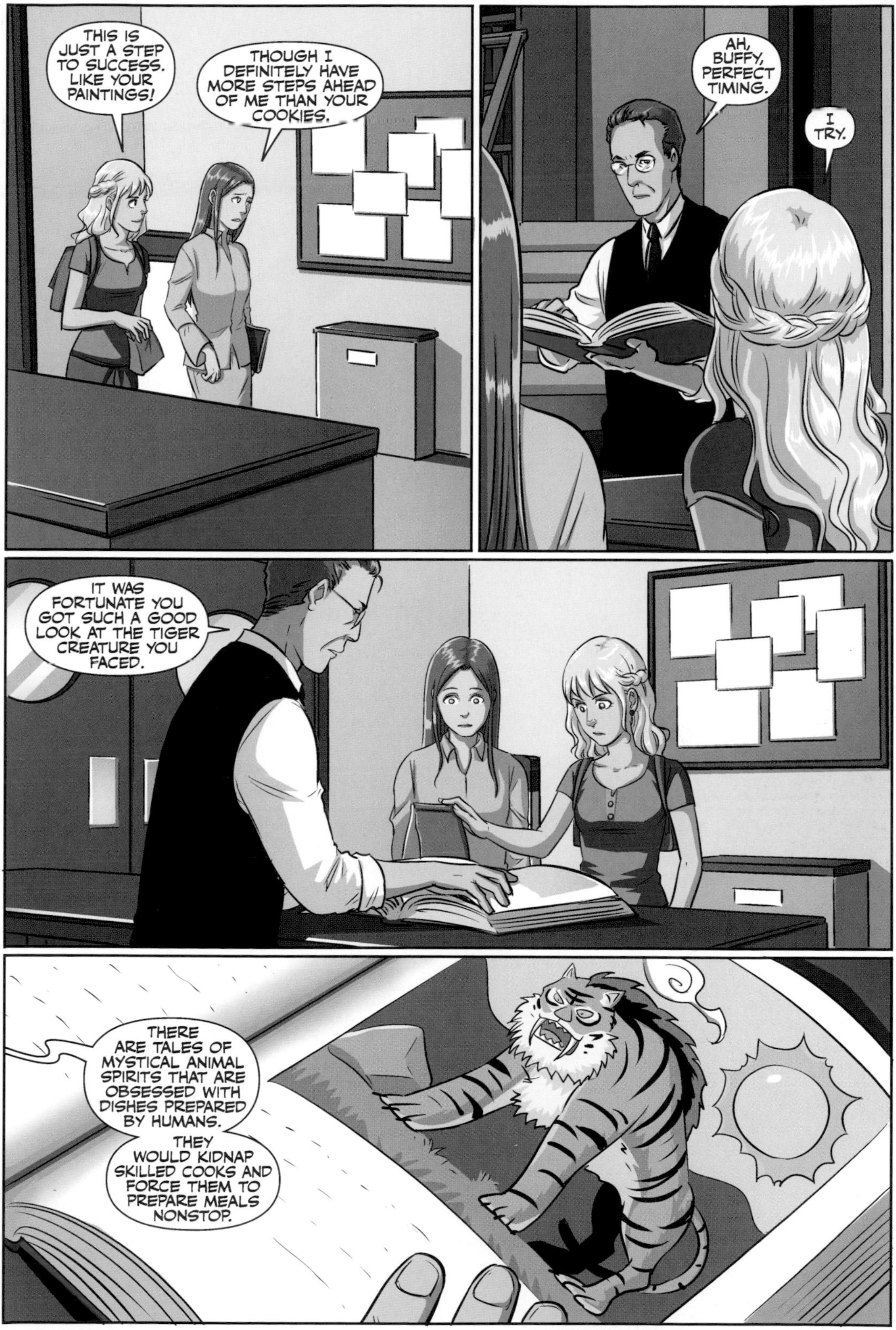
THIS IS JUST A STEP TO SUCCESS. LIKE YOUR PAINTINGS!
THOUGH I DEFINITELY HAVE MORE STEPS AHEAD OF ME THAN YOUR COOKIES.
AH, BUFFY, PERFECT TIMING.
I TRY.
IT WAS FORTUNATE YOU GOT SUCH A GOOD LOOK AT THE TIGER CREATURE YOU FACED.
THERE ARE TALES OF MYSTICAL ANIMAL SPIRITS THAT ARE OBSESSED WITH DISHES PREPARED BY HUMANS.
THEY WOULD KIDNAP SKILLED COOKS AND FORCE THEM TO PREPARE MEALS NONSTOP.

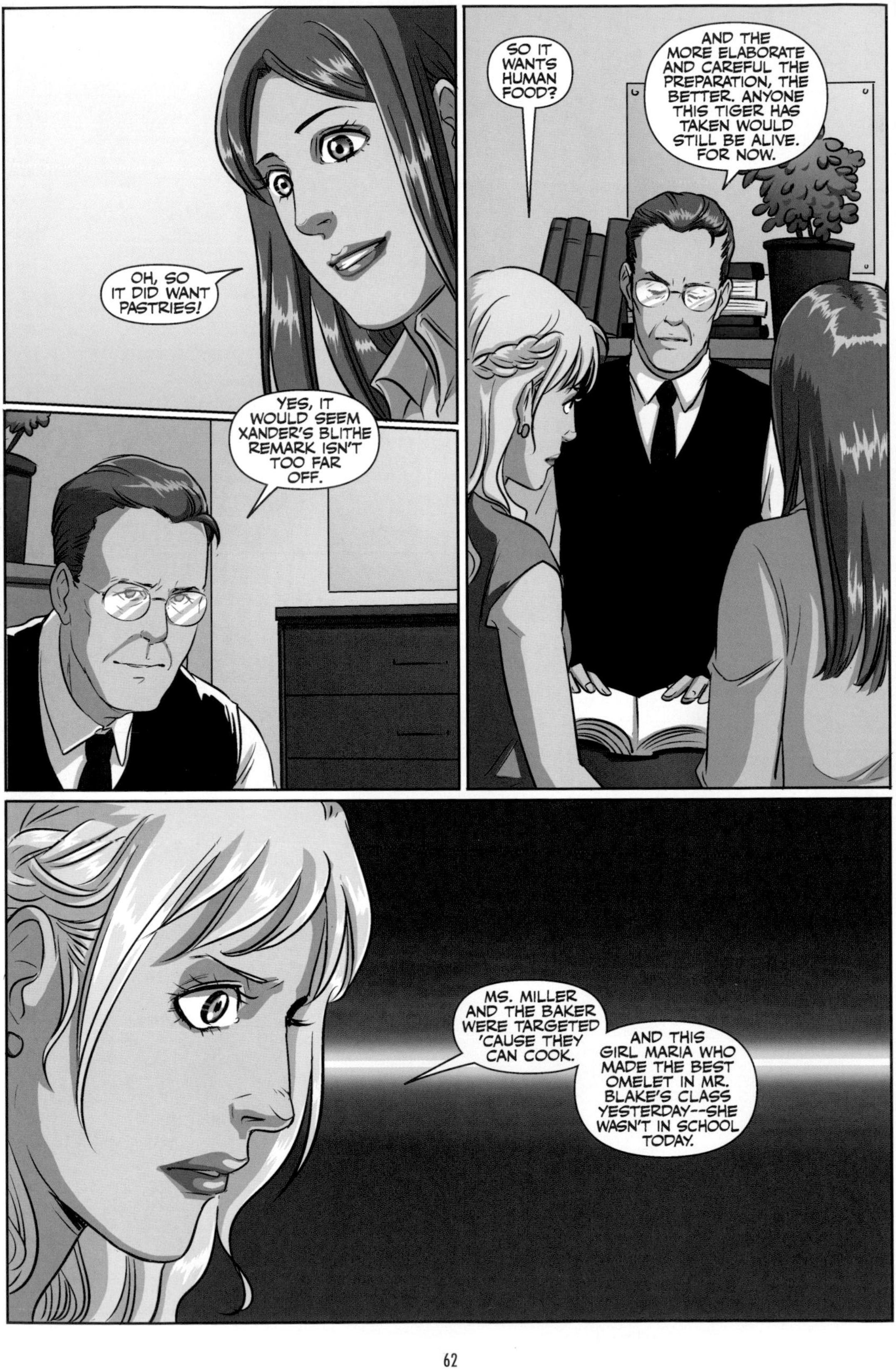
OH, SO IT DID WANT PASTRIES!
SO IT WANTS HUMAN FOOD?
AND THE MORE ELABORATE AND CAREFUL THE PREPARATION, THE BETTER. ANYONE THIS TIGER HAS TAKEN WOULD STILL BE ALIVE. FOR NOW.
YES, IT WOULD SEEM XANDER'S BLITHE REMARK ISN'T TOO FAR OFF.
MS. MILLER AND THE BAKER WERE TARGETED 'CAUSE THEY CAN COOK.
AND THIS GIRL MARIA WHO MADE THE BEST OMELET IN MR. BLAKE'S CLASS YESTERDAY--SHE WASN'T IN SCHOOL TODAY.

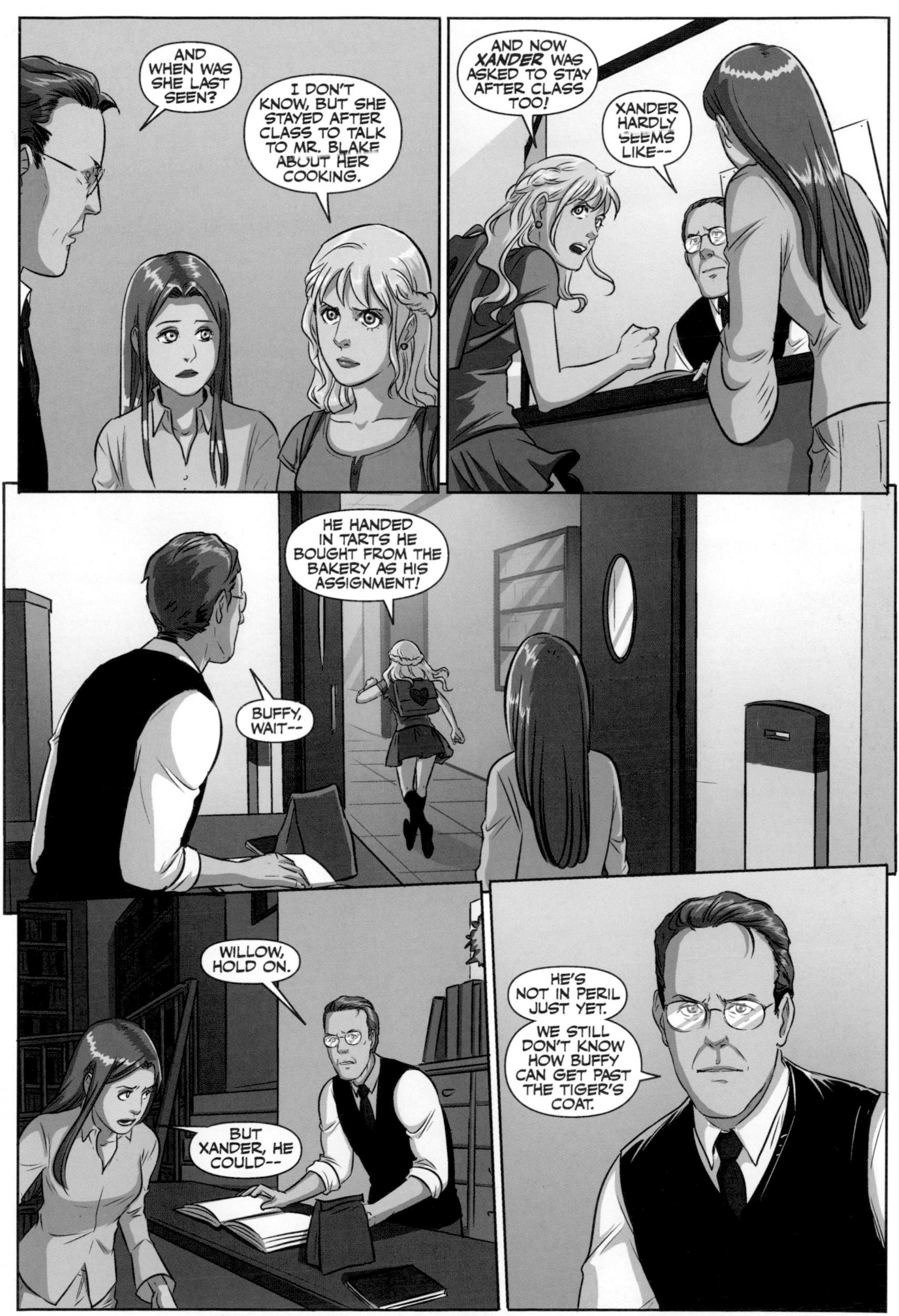
AND WHEN WAS SHE LAST SEEN?
I DON'T KNOW, BUT SHE STAYED AFTER CLASS TO TALK TO MR. BLAKE ABOUT HER COOKING.
AND NOW XANDER WAS ASKED TO STAY AFTER CLASS TOO!
XANDER HARDLY SEEMS LIKE--
HE HANDED IN TARTS HE BOUGHT FROM THE BAKERY AS HIS ASSIGNMENT!
BUFFY, WAIT--
WILLOW, HOLD ON.
BUT XANDER, HE COULD--
HE'S NOT IN PERIL JUST YET.
WE STILL DON'T KNOW HOW BUFFY CAN GET PAST THE TIGER'S COAT.

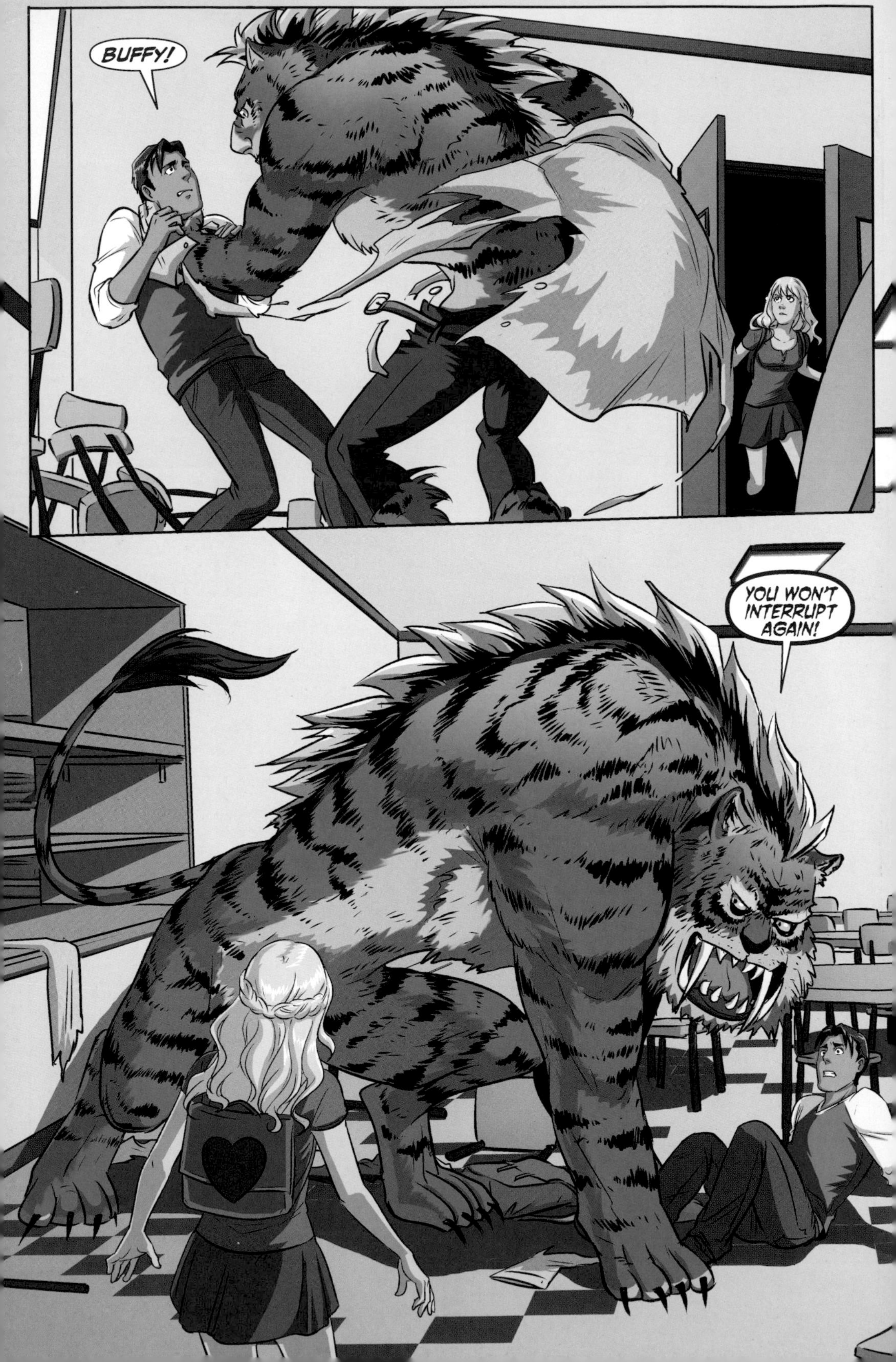
BUFFY!
YOU WON'T INTERRUPT AGAIN!

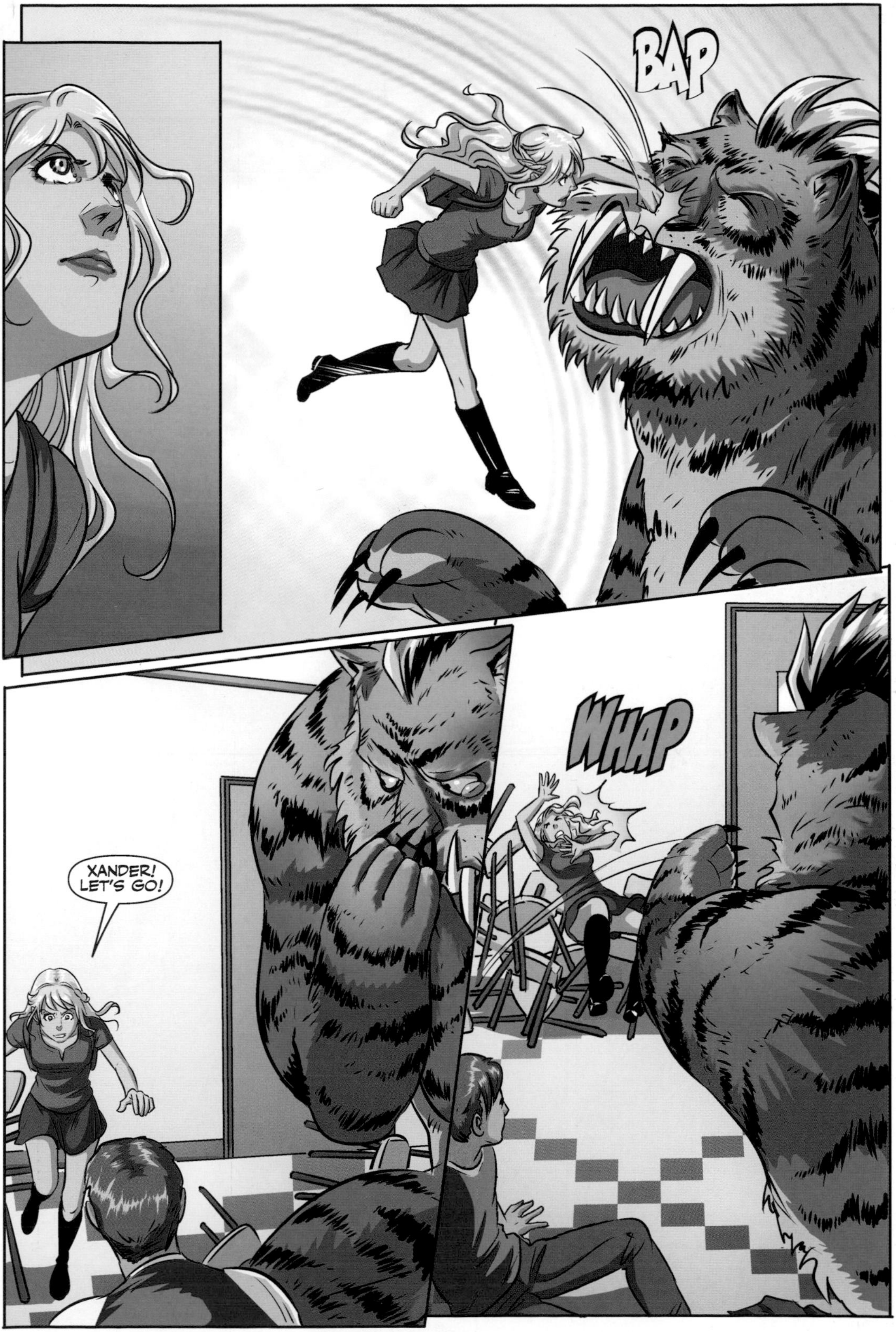
BAP
WHAP
XANDER! LET'S GO!

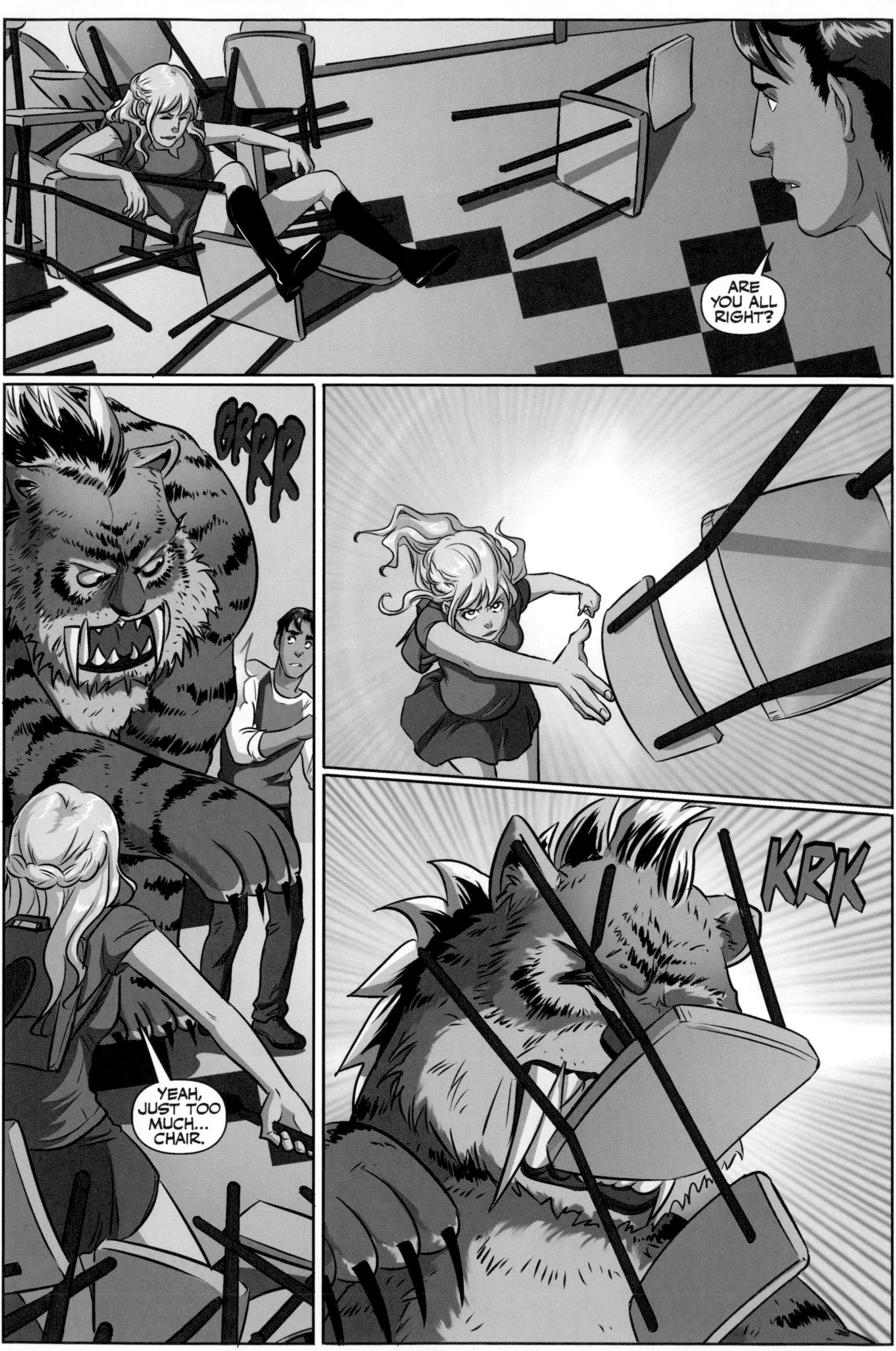

ARE YOU ALL RIGHT?
GRRR
YEAH, JUST TOO MUCH... CHAIR.
KRK

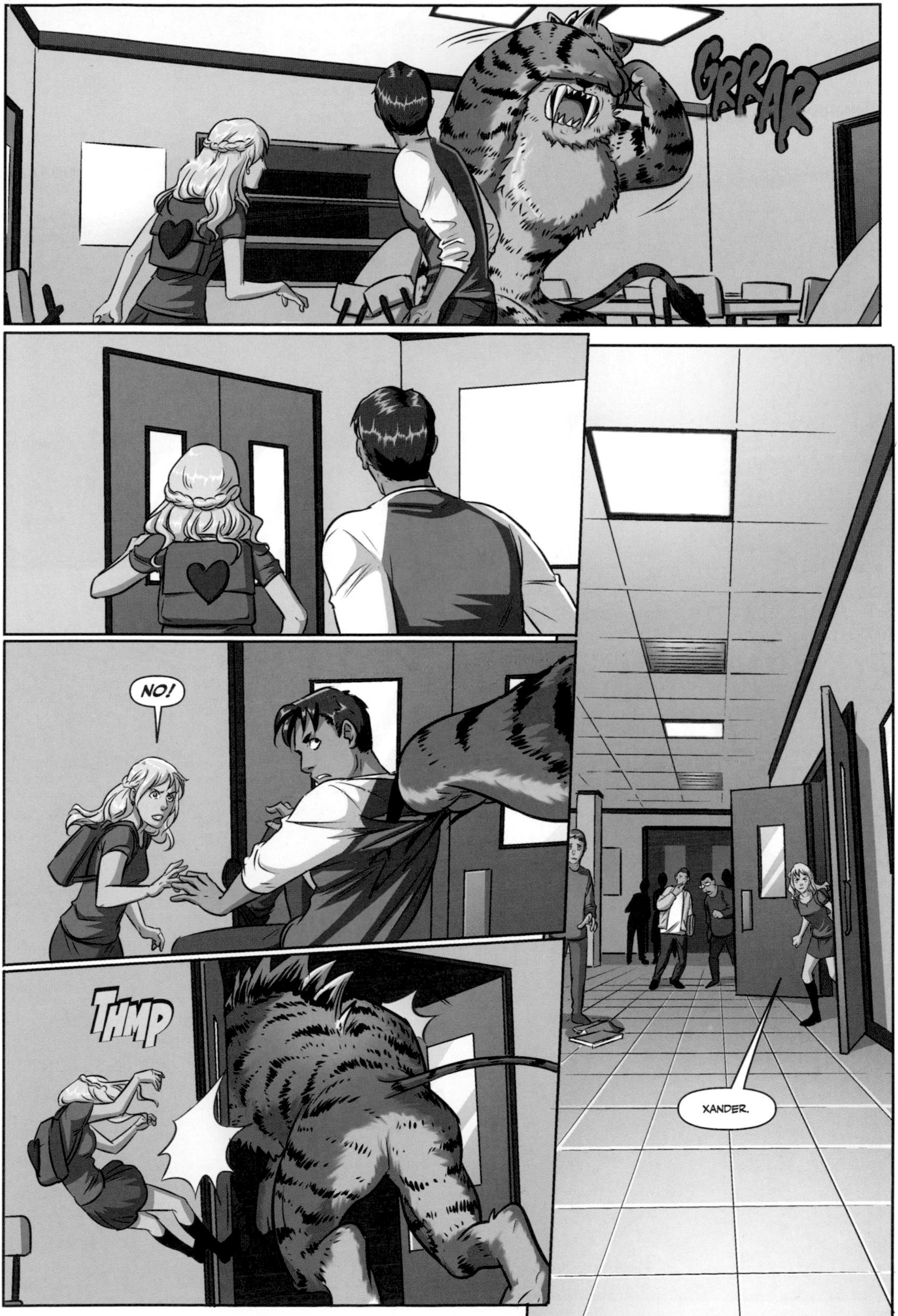
GRRAR
NO!
THMP
XANDER.

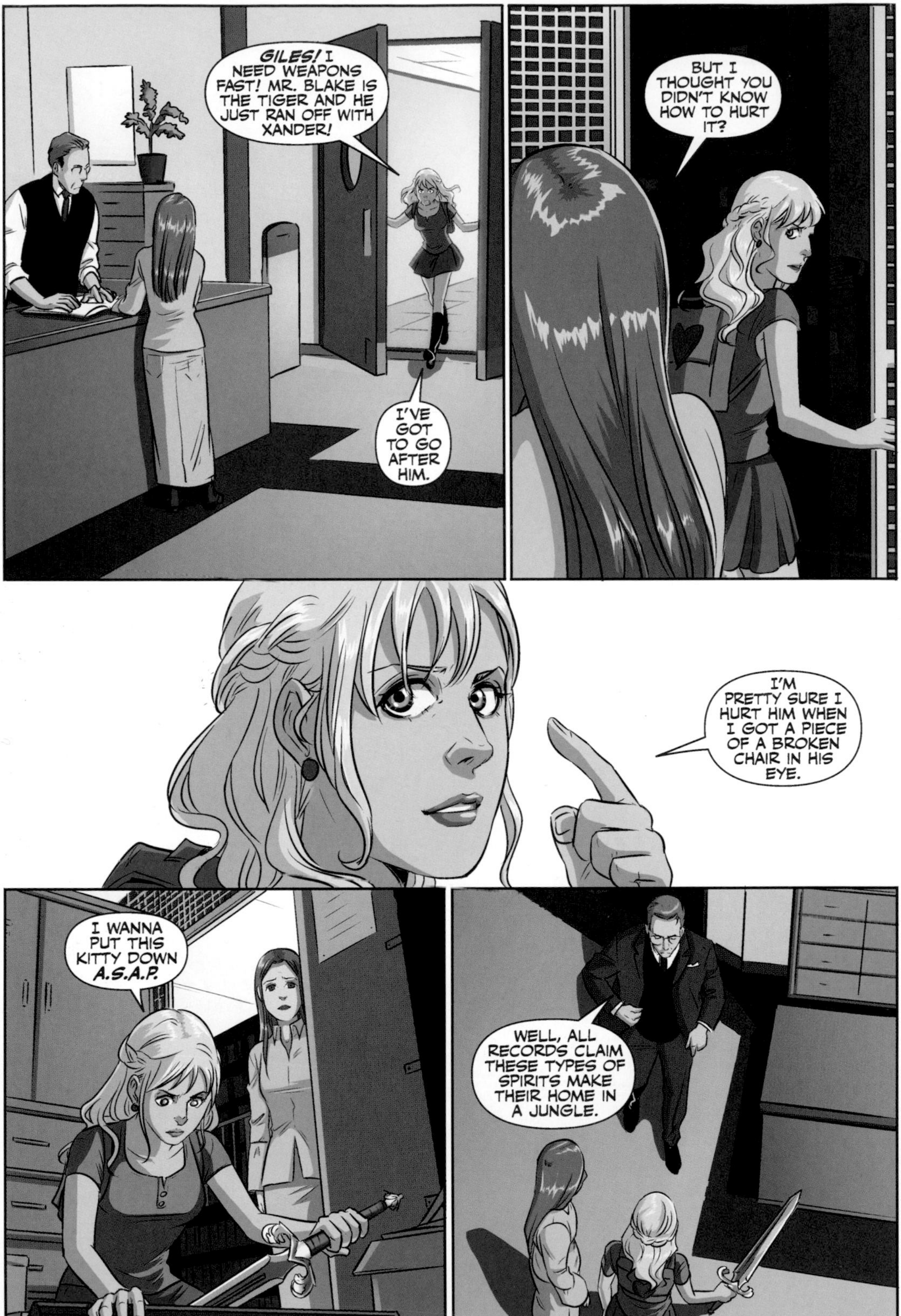
GILES! I NEED WEAPONS FAST! MR. BLAKE IS THE TIGER AND HE JUST RAN OFF WITH XANDER!
I'VE GOT TO GO AFTER HIM.
BUT I THOUGHT YOU DIDN'T KNOW HOW TO HURT IT?
I'M PRETTY SURE I HURT HIM WHEN I GOT A PIECE OF A BROKEN CHAIR IN HIS EYE.
I WANNA PUT THIS KITTY DOWN A.S.A.P.
WELL, ALL RECORDS CLAIM THESE TYPES OF SPIRITS MAKE THEIR HOME IN A JUNGLE.

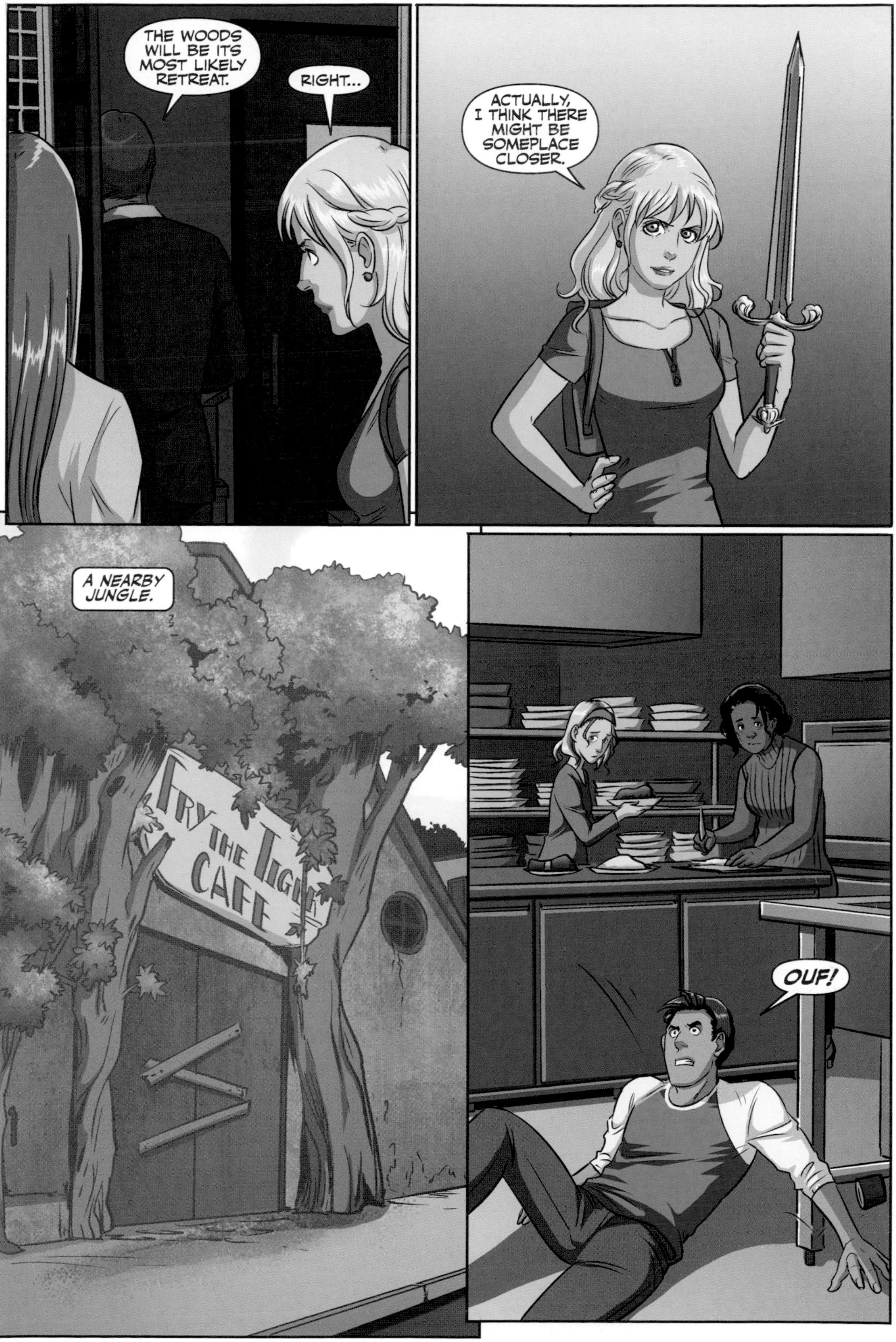
THE WOODS WILL BE ITS MOST LIKELY RETREAT.
RIGHT...
ACTUALLY, I THINK THERE MIGHT BE SOMEPLACE CLOSER.
A NEARBY JUNGLE.
FRY THE TIGER CAFE
OUF!

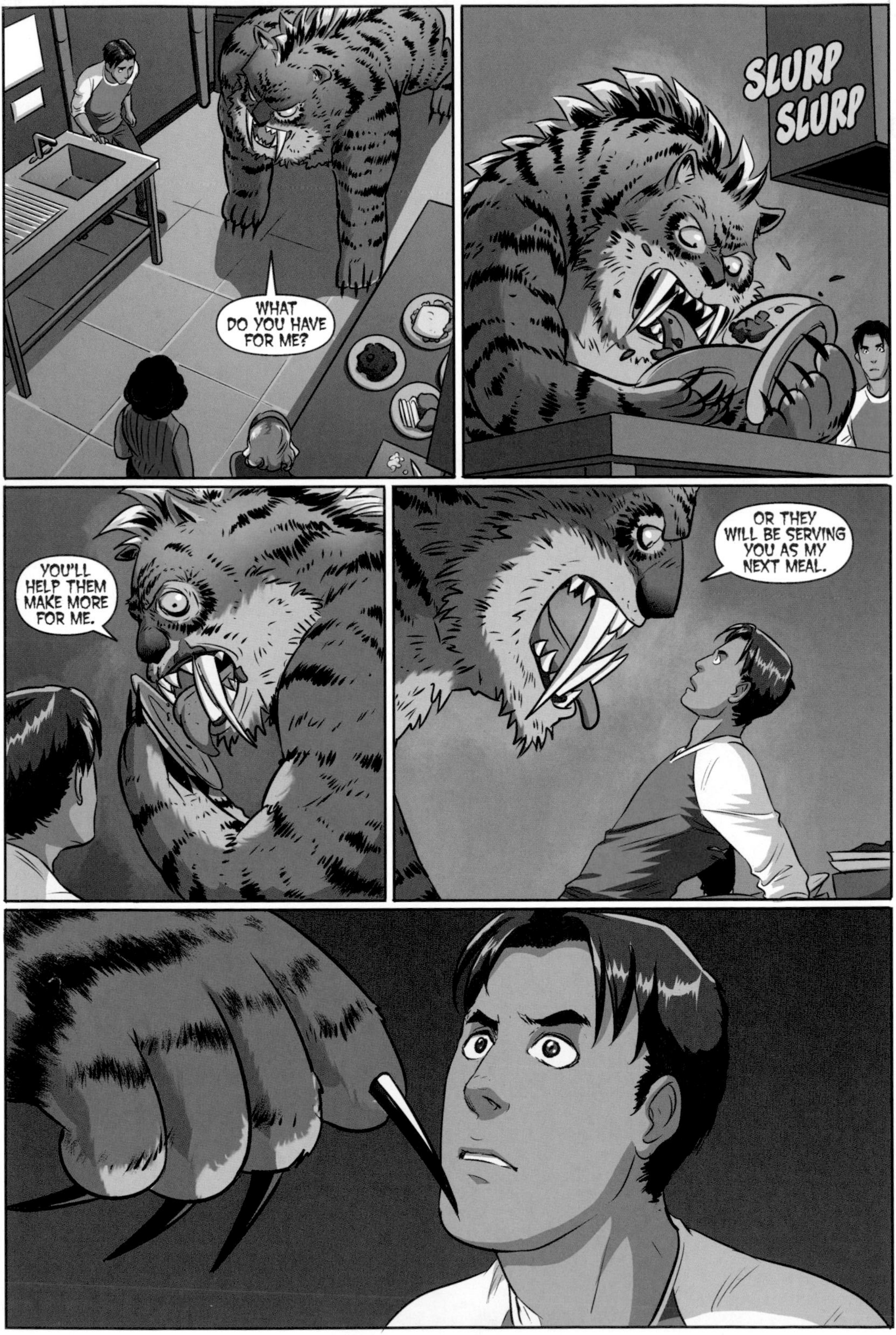
WHAT DO YOU HAVE FOR ME?
SLURP SLURP
YOU'LL HELP THEM MAKE MORE FOR ME.
OR THEY WILL BE SERVING YOU AS MY NEXT MEAL.

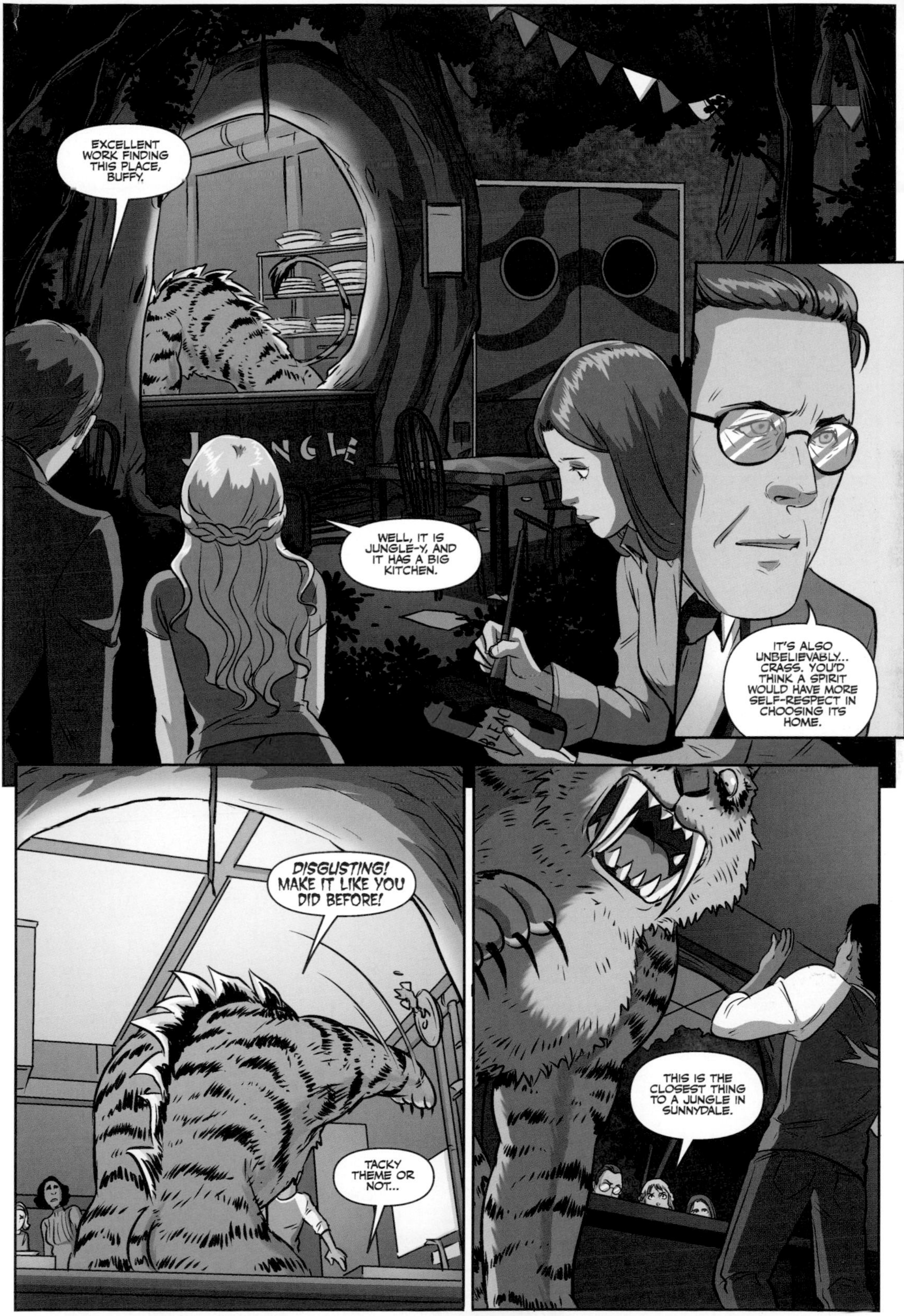
EXCELLENT WORK FINDING THIS PLACE, BUFFY.
JUNGLE
WELL, IT IS JUNGLE-Y, AND IT HAS A BIG KITCHEN.
IT'S ALSO UNBELIEVABLY... CRASS. YOU'D THINK A SPIRIT WOULD HAVE MORE SELF-RESPECT IN CHOOSING ITS HOME.
DISGUSTING! MAKE IT LIKE YOU DID BEFORE!
TACKY THEME OR NOT...
THIS IS THE CLOSEST THING TO A JUNGLE IN SUNNYDALE.

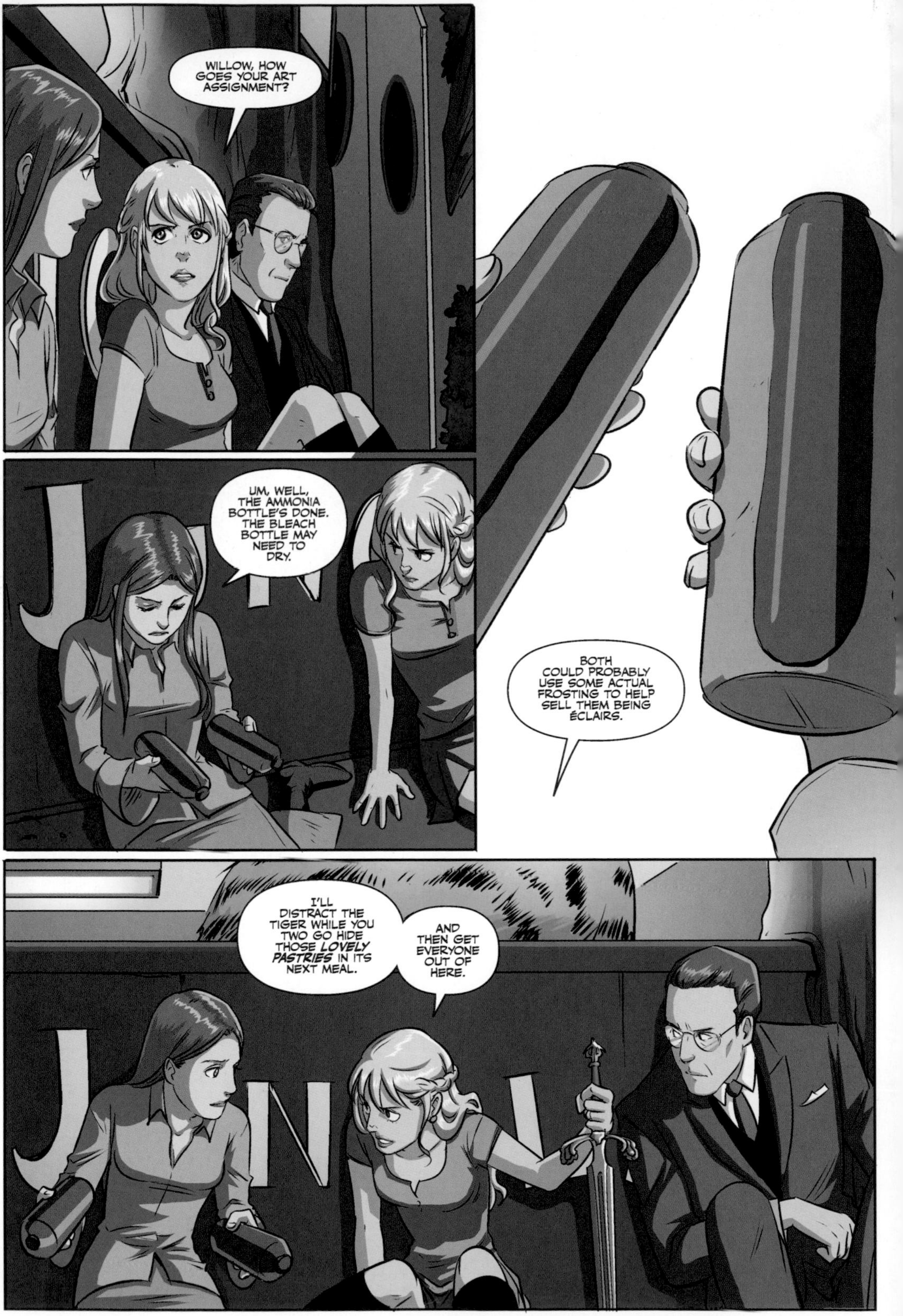
WILLOW, HOW GOES YOUR ART ASSIGNMENT?
UM, WELL, THE AMMONIA BOTTLE'S DONE. THE BLEACH BOTTLE MAY NEED TO DRY.
BOTH COULD PROBABLY USE SOME ACTUAL FROSTING TO HELP SELL THEM BEING ÉCLAIRS.
I'LL DISTRACT THE TIGER WHILE YOU TWO GO HIDE THOSE *LOVELY PASTRIES* IN ITS NEXT MEAL.
AND THEN GET EVERYONE OUT OF HERE.

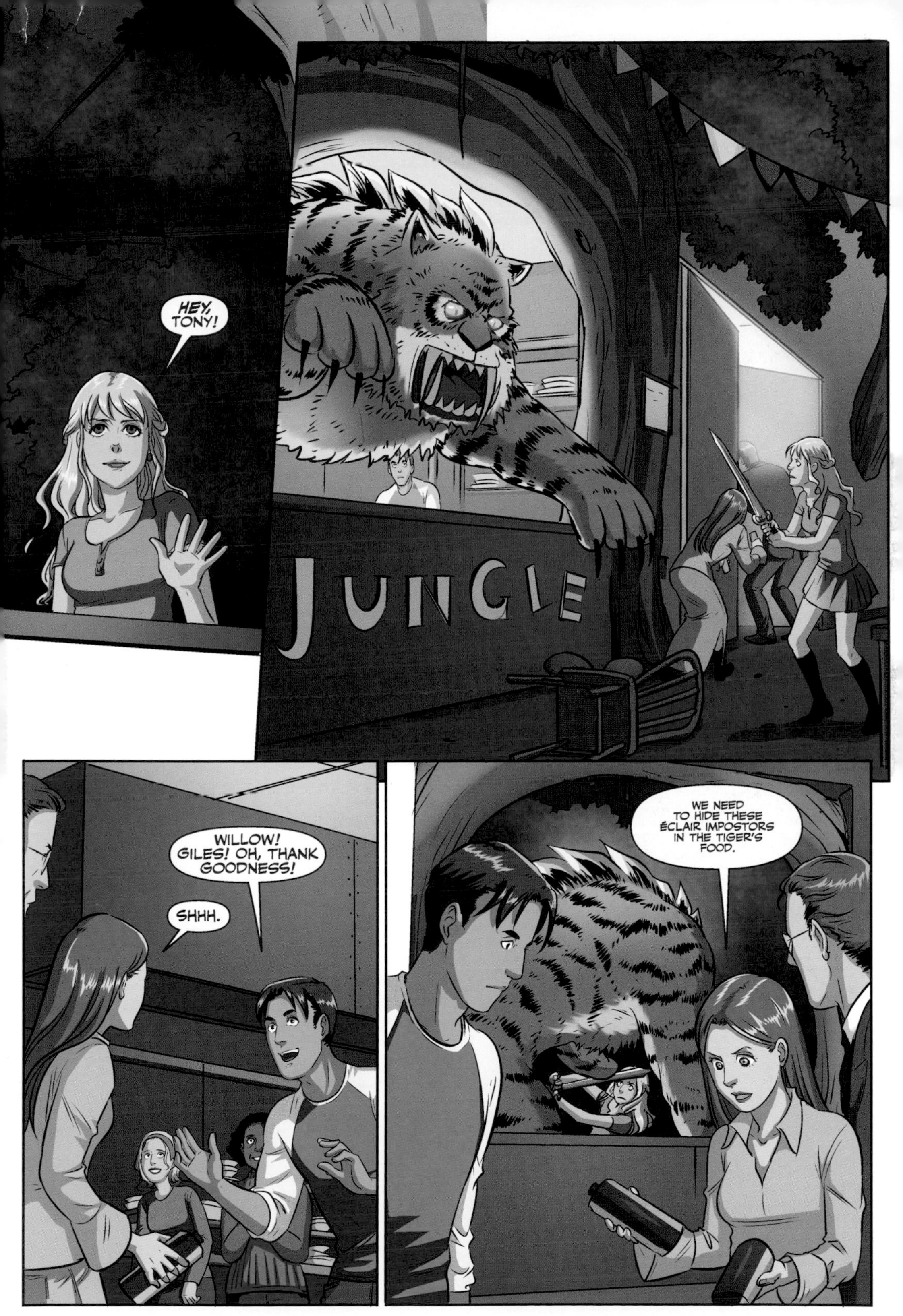
HEY, TONY!
JUNGLE
WILLOW! GILES! OH, THANK GOODNESS!
SHHH.
WE NEED TO HIDE THESE ÉCLAIR IMPOSTORS IN THE TIGER'S FOOD.

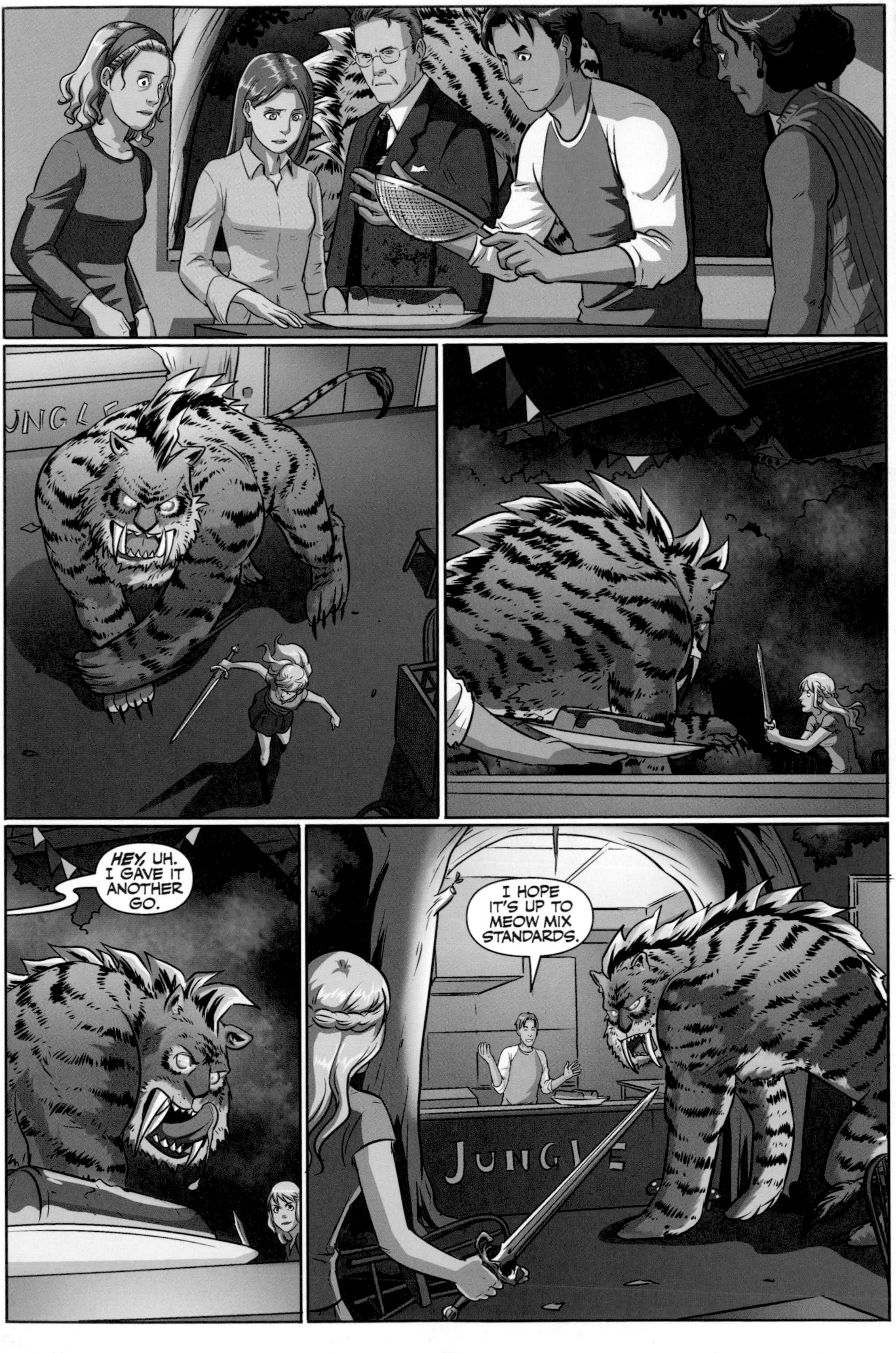
UNGLE
HEY, UH. I GAVE IT ANOTHER GO.
I HOPE IT'S UP TO MEOW MIX STANDARDS.
JUNGLE

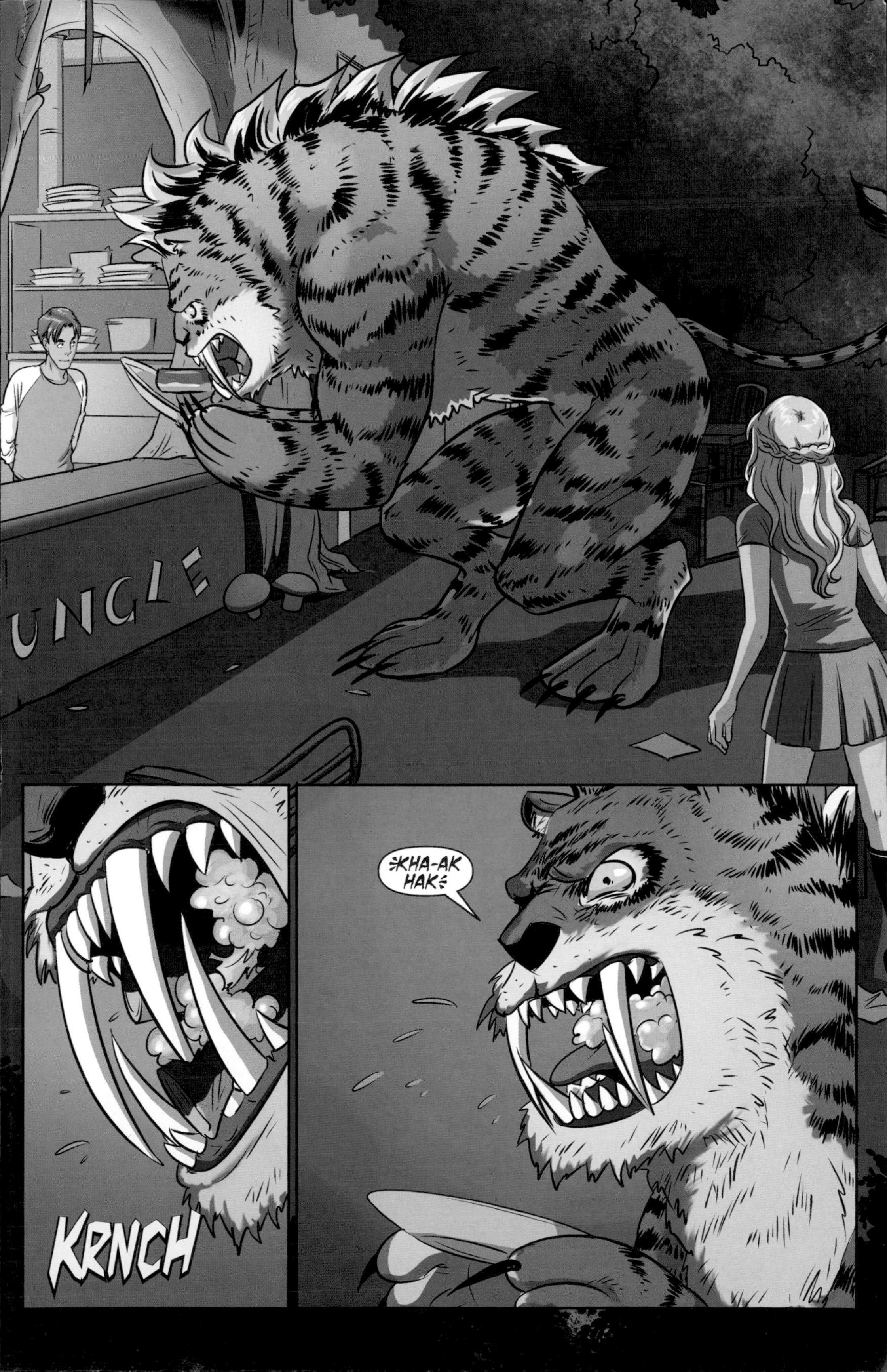
UNGLE
KRNCH
KHA-AK HAK

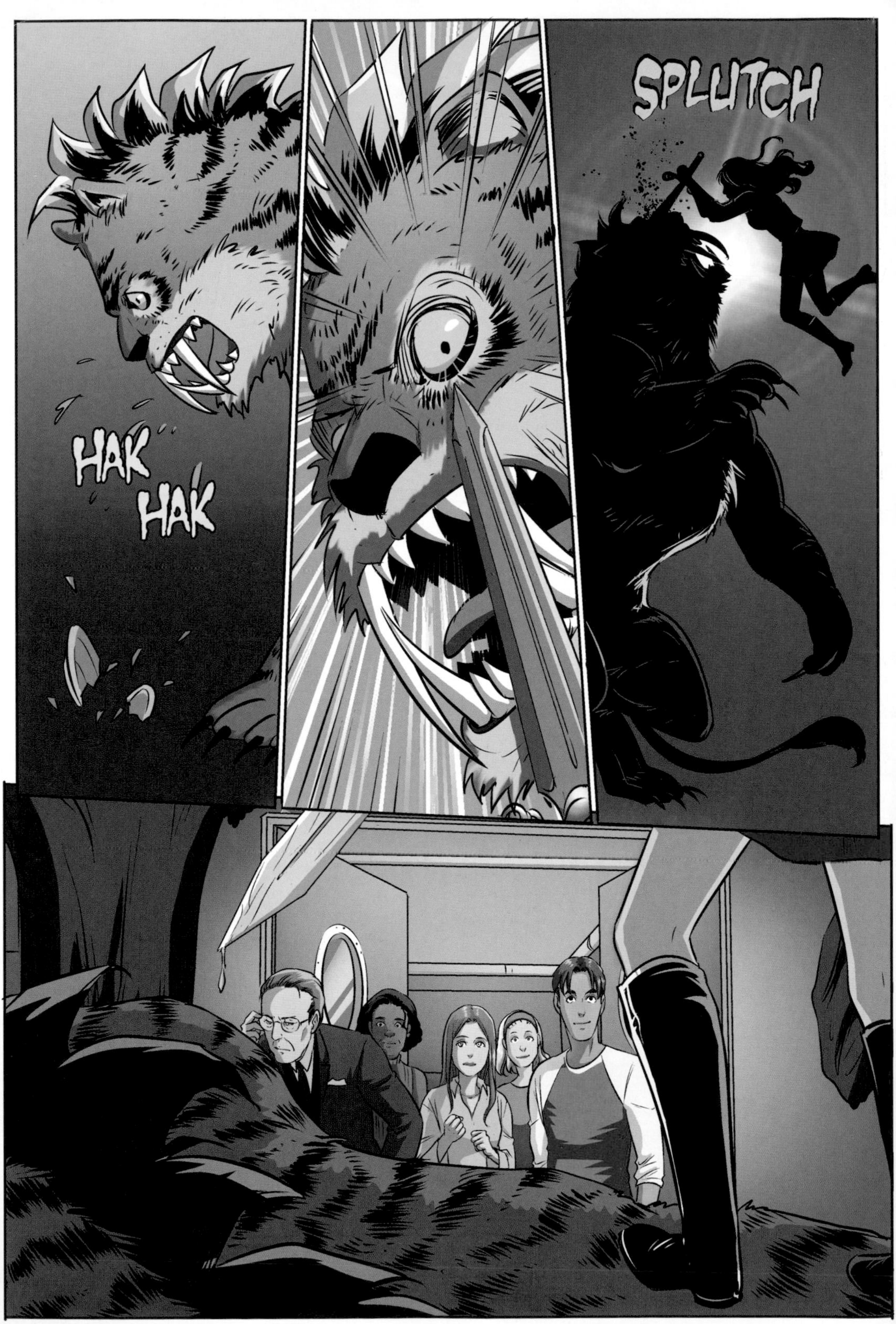
HAK
HAK
SPLUTCH

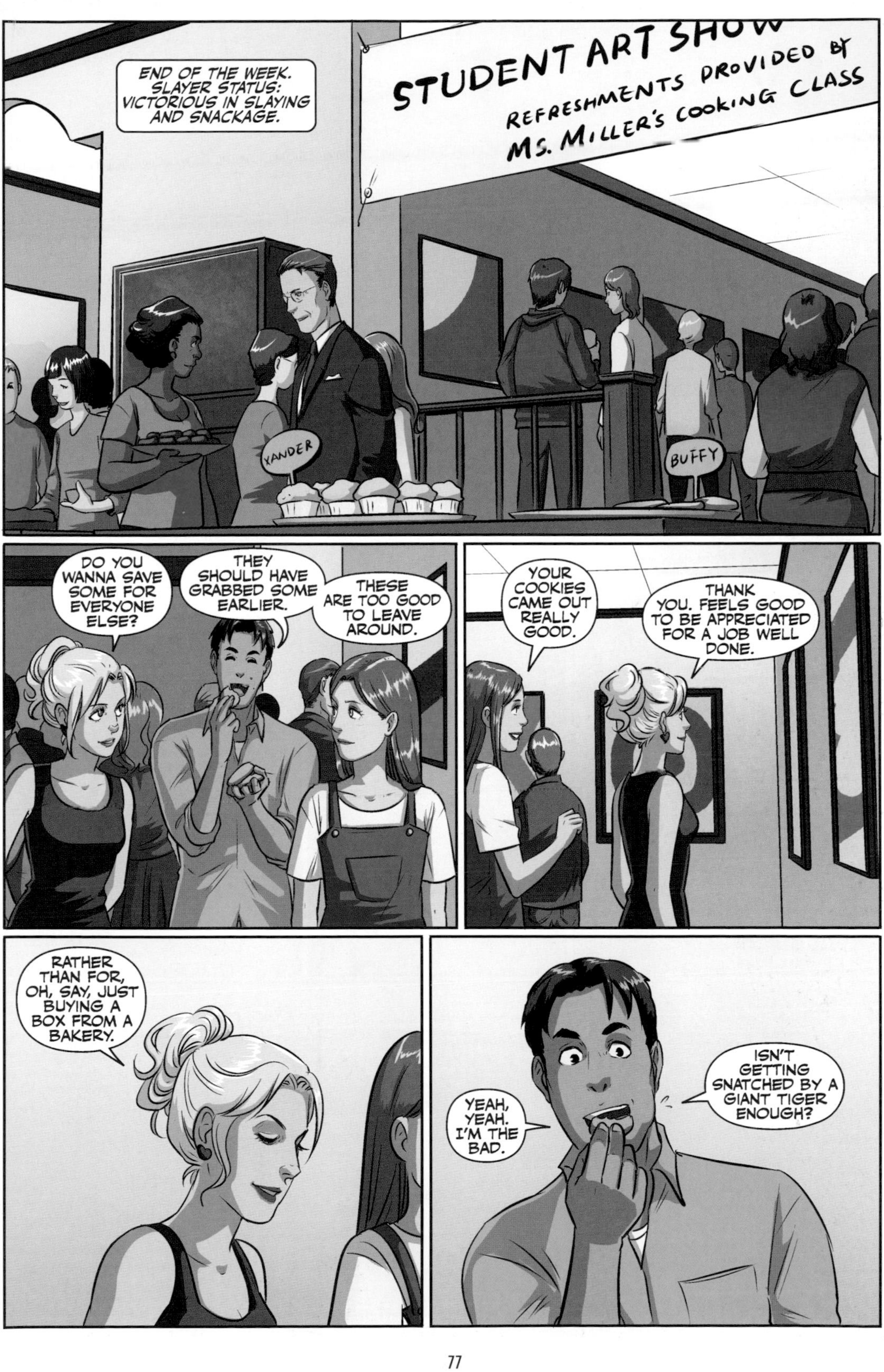

END OF THE WEEK. SLAYER STATUS: VICTORIOUS IN SLAYING AND SNACKAGE.
STUDENT ART SHOW
REFRESHMENTS PROVIDED BY MS. MILLER'S COOKING CLASS
XANDER
BUFFY
DO YOU WANNA SAVE SOME FOR EVERYONE ELSE?
THEY SHOULD HAVE GRABBED SOME EARLIER.
THESE ARE TOO GOOD TO LEAVE AROUND.
YOUR COOKIES CAME OUT REALLY GOOD.
THANK YOU. FEELS GOOD TO BE APPRECIATED FOR A JOB WELL DONE.
RATHER THAN FOR, OH, SAY, JUST BUYING A BOX FROM A BAKERY.
YEAH, YEAH. I'M THE BAD.
ISN'T GETTING SNATCHED BY A GIANT TIGER ENOUGH?

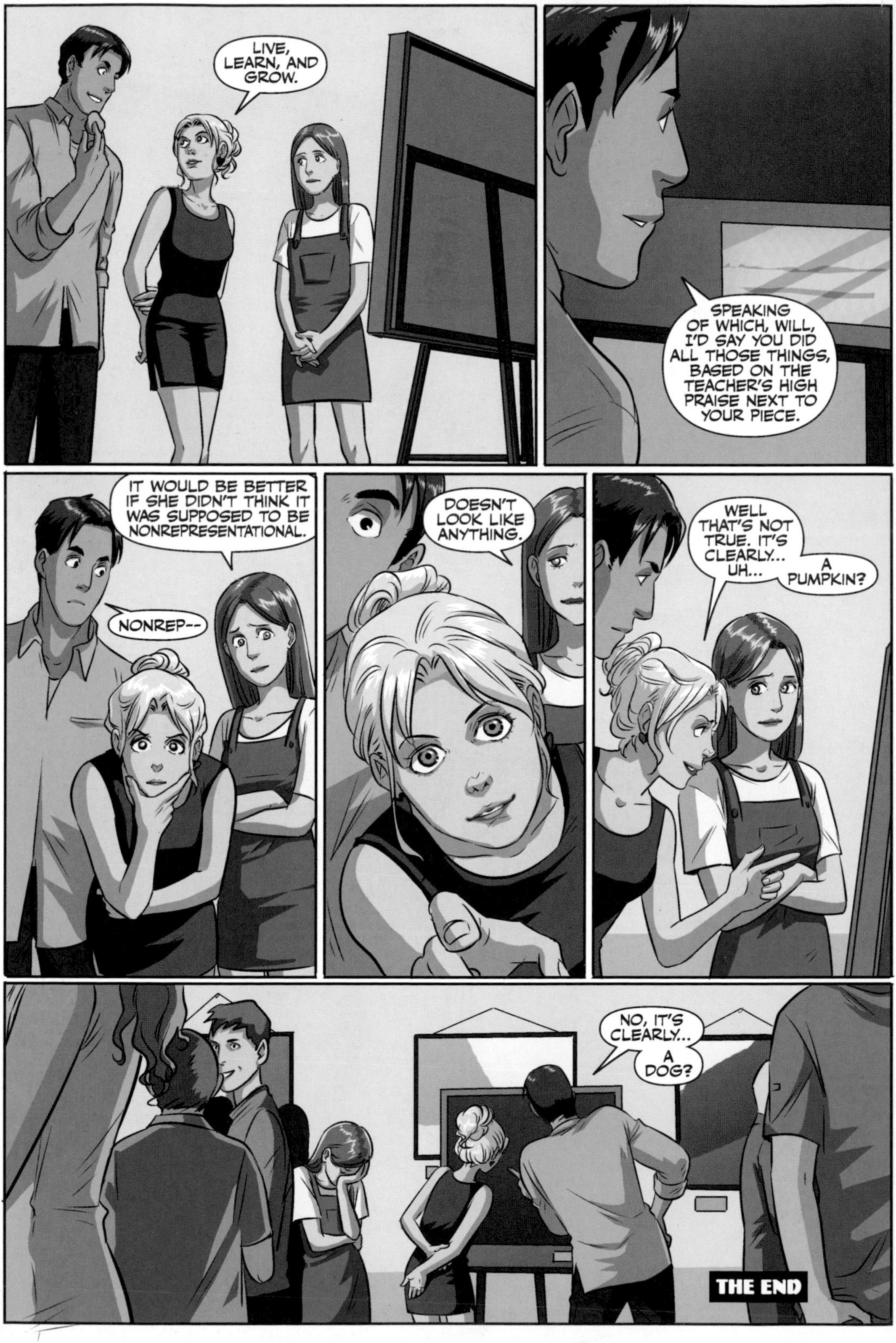
LIVE, LEARN, AND GROW.
SPEAKING OF WHICH, WILL, I'D SAY YOU DID ALL THOSE THINGS, BASED ON THE TEACHER'S HIGH PRAISE NEXT TO YOUR PIECE.
IT WOULD BE BETTER IF SHE DIDN'T THINK IT WAS SUPPOSED TO BE NONREPRESENTATIONAL.
NONREP--
DOESN'T LOOK LIKE ANYTHING.
WELL THAT'S NOT TRUE. IT'S CLEARLY... UH...
A PUMPKIN?
NO, IT'S CLEARLY...
A DOG?
THE END